Having *faith*

—— One Woman's Nine-Year Faith Journey from Infertility to Motherhood ——

Nicole Zoch

LIONIZE
— *Press* —

Having *faith*

Published by Lionize Press

Edited by Jeanette Windle

Cover Design by Simon Burnett, Univer Digital

Cover by Kim Selby Photography

Contents

Contents

Acknowledgements

"Give thanks in all circumstances; for this is God's will for you in Christ Jesus." –1 Thessalonians 5:18

Having Faith has only been achieved because of the direction that the Holy Spirit gave me as I was writing. God is the inspiration for this book, and I give him all the glory and honor for encouraging me to record my barrenness-to-freedom journey on paper. Jesus is the Author and Perfecter of our faith (Hebrews 12:2), and in that sense he is also the true Author of this book since my life of faith chronicled in the following pages comes only through his working in my life and heart.

In this acknowledgement, I would like to thank my wonderful, supportive husband, Jamie. You have been the strength and prayer behind this book, and I am forever grateful for your friendship, love, and devotion throughout our difficult journey. Thank you for your knowledge of the Bible. You have always encouraged me to stand firm in our belief in the miracle of conception, reiterating this time and again through faithful prayer and words of wisdom. I am so blessed to do life with such a man as you.

To Bob and Jan Osborne, our long-time mentors and faithful spiritual warriors, thank you for journeying this walk with us so fervently. Without your insight, reliability, encouragement, and obedience to God, we would have struggled to persevere to the end.

To my editor Jeanette Windle, thank you, truly! The truthfulness and honesty you brought to assessing my work was a God-send. And your comprehension of Scripture: enormously valuable. I do not think this book would be what it is today under any other tutelage. God has used your gifts and talents to polish this book beautifully.

–Acknowledgement–

And to our pastor and friend, Simon Burnett, thank you for not only encouraging me to believe in my God-given purpose, but for inspiring me to embrace the calling that is upon my life as well.

Thank you also for the amazing cover design you created for Having Faith and for supporting me in the business-end of this project. You have been invaluable in bringing my story to print, and I am so thankful God placed you in my life.

Lastly, to our family and friends who prayed continuously for us to receive the gift of children, thank you from the bottom of our hearts. Revelations 5:8 tells us that prayer is like sweet incense to God. He loves our prayers. We needed your prayers. In response to all of them, our dream of becoming parents became a reality.

Dedication

Jesus said: "Let the little children come to me, and do not hinder

them, for the kingdom of heaven belongs to such as these."

– Matthew 19:14

This book, my darling children, is a demonstration of our adoring love for each one of you even before you were born. It is also a manifestation of the faithful love of a Father in heaven who has fulfilled our dream in having you. This book is because of you and devoted to each one of you.

Faith, you are our beautiful, effervescent song-bird and the firstborn fruit of our faith journey. You have captivated us from day one. Joel, our handsome man around the house, you have a servant's heart, and we are so proud of the young man you have become. And Levi, your loving smile and cheeky ways have mesmerized us all. You are truly awesome and perfectly complete our family.

We love all of you so very much and praise God for entrusting us with the parenting of each one of you—his precious children.

Introduction

"Children are a heritage of the Lord, offspring a reward from him." – Psalm 127:3

From as young as I can remember, I have had the simple desire of becoming a mum. In fact, throughout my childhood I really didn't aspire for a career. I only ever wanted to be a wife and mother. I thought these roles were the ultimate appointment, and I desired such a life more than anything.

I was born in December, 1976, my mother of German descent and my father of Austrian. My parents migrated to Australia from Europe with their own families when they were both still young. My Dad's family arrived in April 1955, whilst my mother's family ended their immigrant boat-voyage five-years later. Both families

7

settled in the small industrial seaside town of Wollongong about an hour south of Sydney.

Dad and Mum met at their local high school. My mother was just fourteen when she fell in love with a handsome Austrian four years her senior. They married soon after Mum completed high school. In the early 1970s, they moved away from their hometown of Wollongong, settling in Canberra, Australia's capital city, where my two older brothers and I were born a few years later.

I had a very happy childhood, filled with all the lovely warmth and comfort any child could wish. My parents were doting, and my brothers were my heroes. We moved quite a lot, including from Canberra to Sydney, the capital of New South Wales on Australia's east coast, when I was ten, then two years later to Brisbane, Queensland, another coastal city about a thousand kilometers north of Sydney. Since we were a close-knit family, these moves only strengthened our bond with each other.

My family belonged to an unconventional church group which among other distinctives observed many Jewish holidays. We would periodically celebrate some of these festivals with other churches within our denomination around Australia. This made moving to a new city easier as our family already had church friendship connections throughout the Australian continent.

Although I knew our church was different and that other churches might consider its doctrinal positions eccentric, as a child I was proud of the church to which I belonged, and I completely trusted and lived out the faith convictions I was taught. It was not until my early adulthood that I discovered these religious beliefs I'd lived and breathed were actually false. That discovery would cause everything I'd held as a true foundation to my life to come unglued (more on this later).

Growing up in Australia in the eighties felt mostly safe and free. It was the era when Rubik's Cubes, Yoyos, and Coca Cola were all the rage. Color television was the new norm, and videos were introduced. We children read and lived out in our backyards books like the Magic Faraway Tree and the Famous Five by Enid Blyton. It was a time in my life when I was carefree and almost everything felt good and right.

It was also during this time period that I developed a passion for romantic movies and fanciful love stories. So it is little wonder that by the time I met my own beau, I had already formed a strong idealism about what I expected in a relationship. I was fifteen years old in January, 1992, when I first met Jamie Zoch, a 23-year-old carpenter from Sunbury, Victoria. At the time, this was a small farming community, but it has since grown to be a satellite city of the Greater Melbourne metropolitan area.

Melbourne itself is sixteen-hundred kilometers south of where I lived in Brisbane on the southern coast of Australia. If you are reading this in some other country and have noticed that every city I mention seems to be along the coast, that is indeed the case for all of Australia's major cities. In fact, 98% of Australia's almost twenty-five million residents live within a hundred kilometers of the coast, leaving Australia's famed Outback interior largely unpopulated.

On this particular long weekend, my family had been invited to attend a wedding out on a picturesque lakeside estate about ninety minutes' drive southwest of Brisbane. At fifteen, I was growing more independent all the time, so I decided to head off to the wedding with a girlfriend who was being picked up by Jamie. In fact, she was the one who had invited Jamie to this wedding when they'd met several months earlier at an annual church camp our denomination held for its youth and young adults.

I had seen pictures of Jamie, my friend's guest, and thought him very handsome with a strong resemblance to the movie star Richard Gere. I had also heard he was quite the gentleman. As I had secretly hoped, Jamie and I had a strong connection from our first encounter. In fact, as he would tell it, it was love at first sight.

Jamie and I spent much of that wedding weekend getting to know each other. As we chatted, laughed, and generally enjoyed each other's company, we discovered that we shared the same ambitions, desires, and morals. Having grown up in the same church denomination, we also held a common belief system.

Jamie even found my romantic, feminine, and idealistic notions fascinating and appealing to his more rugged, masculine nature. There was no doubt fireworks sparked between us that weekend. But with our eight-year age difference and sixteen-hundred kilometers separating our worlds, I had no expectation of any further relationship and indeed accepted that we would go our separate ways at the end of the weekend.

But just a few months later, our worlds again aligned at a church ball in my home city of Brisbane. In our denomination, it was quite common to travel long distances cross-country to attend dances and other activities hosted by other member churches. And I knew Jamie would be attending this particular dance since he'd already invited the same girlfriend with whom I'd traveled to the wedding to be his partner for this dance back before I even met him. Still, it was a breathless moment for me when my eyes met Jamie's on the night of the ball, and I will never forget the smile that lit up his face when he spotted me. Or how perfect it felt to be in his arms when he asked me to dance with him.

We met one more time that year at an annual week-long church festival on the Gold Coast, the Australian equivalent to Hawaii's Waikiki Beach. I knew Jamie was also planning to attend the festival, so I was greatly anticipating seeing him again. During that week, Jamie and

I often sought each other out after church services or at other activities. While we enjoyed each other's company enormously, I returned home once again with no expectation of anything more.

But unbeknownst to me, Jamie was far more interested in me than I had realized. I must admit this was rather naïve on my part! But by the following summer, he made his intentions toward me quite clear. I've mentioned before the annual youth camp our denomination organized, which was where Jamie had met my girlfriend who'd introduced us to each other. The camp was in a small country town in Victoria about a half-hour drive from where Jamie lived near Melbourne.

This particular summer vacation in December, 1992 (for northern readers, keep in mind that Australia is south of the equator, so December is full summer), I applied to go as a camper. Meanwhile, Jamie had been trying to conjure a plan to somehow meet me again. When he got wind that I would be attending camp, he registered as a camp waterski instructor so he could see me again. By the end of summer camp, we had both fallen deeply in love. Jamie declared his feelings towards me, which became the start of a two-and-a-half-year courtship. To me, it was also the beginning of my very own fairytale love story and what I believed would be my happily-ever-after.

I have always been—and continue to be—a hopeless romantic. I am drawn to eras of yesteryear, particularly to the 1920s and 1940s when men would woo and a lady would swoon. I love romantic novels and movies, adore anything Parisian, and during my own courting years watched every romantic movie I think was ever produced. This, of course, filled my head with fictitious love stories.

In my younger years before I met Jamie, my dad and I would often stay up late, listening to Dad's old-time music or watching classic black-and-white movies with beautiful stars like Ginger Rogers, Debbie Reynolds, and Doris Day.

While we watched, Dad and I would chat about my future wedding and all that I wanted it to be. We would also have long chats about the type of man I wanted to marry.

Yes, in my childhood fantasy I had it all figured out. I would simply meet and fall in love with a handsome Prince Charming, just like the movie stars did in all of their movies. I would get married, start a family, and live happily ever after. What I failed to notice was that in all those romantic books or movies some less-than-happy drama always unfolded somewhere in the middle of the storyline. My own love story would prove no different.

For our first year following that summer camp when Jamie declared his intentions to me, we endured a long-distance relationship with Jamie in Victoria and me in Brisbane. But saying goodbye after each fleeting visit had become increasingly difficult, and it became evident that if Jamie wanted to date me more consistently and pursue a deeper relationship, he would need to move to Brisbane. So at the end of 1994, Jamie moved to Brisbane, where he found a job in the construction industry.

During this same period, I had begun studies as a legal secretary. Due to skipping a grade when we'd moved to Brisbane, where my school was much easier than in Sydney, I'd graduated high school at sixteen and was only seventeen when I finished my secretarial training and began working in a Brisbane law firm, followed soon after by secretarial work in the hotel industry on the Gold Coast.

On the side, I was also dabbling a little in modelling. This career venture proved relatively short-lived, partly due to the demands the modelling agency placed upon me, but mostly because the type of work I was attracting didn't fit with my Christian ethos at all. So apart from a few catwalks, promotional work, and a handful of photoshoots, most of my work was secretarial.

With Jamie and me now in the same city, our personal relationship also continued to blossom, making a marriage proposal inevitable. Just twenty months after Jamie moved to Brisbane, on August 6, 1995, my father walked me down the aisle to my husband-to-be. It was a beautiful, if rather chilly, outdoor garden wedding on the Gold Coast. There in front of about seventy close friends and family, Jamie and I exchanged wedding vows and publicly declared our love and devotion to each other.

But though Jamie and I had spoken all the right vows during our marriage ceremony, for me these were just words, something you did at a wedding. I was still so very young, only eighteen when we married. I had fulfilled my childhood fantasy of marrying Prince Charming. In fact, with Jamie I'd ticked off every box on my idealistic husband list. But I had never considered what *forever*, the obvious result of marriage, really meant. After all, most movies end once the couple gets married, so you rarely see what comes next.

My first big hurdle was leaving my home and family. While Jamie had moved to Brisbane to be near me, we had always seen his move as temporary since his father owned a building company back in Victoria, where Jamie would have the security of a guaranteed job. Jamie also owned a house there, which he'd built some years earlier and had been renting out while he was living in Brisbane. It had always been our intention once we were married to move back to Victoria to live in his house and work at his father's company.

So just six months after our wedding day, Jamie and I packed up and moved two states away from my family and friends. I was now nineteen years old, and I saw moving as a huge adventure. I was also intoxicated by the life voyage on which I'd embarked.

Never did I consider that perhaps I wasn't ready for marriage, let alone a life away from my closest friends and supportive family. And being so young and naive, I never stopped to consider either how the very different upbringings Jamie and I had experienced might play a part in our marriage union. As superficial as this sounds, I had actually considered nothing beyond our wedding day.

So when Jamie and I moved to Victoria in early 1996, I didn't just have to grapple with moving from Brisbane suburbia to a small country town in a different state, but I also had to adjust to a new family that was vastly different from my own. Added to that was a new friendship circle Jamie had known all his life but was unfamiliar to me and also much older, due to our eight-year difference in age. Beyond that, I also had to contend with what turned out to be completely different outlooks on marriage.

You see, while Jamie and I grew up in the same church denomination with a similar belief system, our family expectations were not similar at all. I held a very unrealistic view of marriage, expecting to do everything as a couple. In contrast, Jamie had grown up very self-sufficient and was used to doing things on his own. We were poles apart in our expectations of marriage, which caused a wedge in our relationship.

Our completely different outlook on marriage was actually something the minister who married us had discussed in length and out of concern during our pre-wedding counseling. The counseling included a marriage preparation course that asked multiple questions designed to establish partner compatibility and comprehension of the vows we were about to take. I went into the questionnaire feeling confident and expecting to do well.

Conversely, I anticipated a big fail for Jamie, since in my opinion I communicated love much better than Jamie. I expected the test results to prove this and show up Jamie's shortfalls. As it turned out, nothing was further from the truth. In fact, my own test results were quite alarming; a story Jamie still enjoys recalling at many a dinner party.

The results were marked within two circles. There was an inner circle, an outer circle, then the rest of the page. The closer you got to within the inner circle, the more prepared and realistic you were for marriage. Jamie was not only within the inner circle but had nearly a bullseye. He was well prepared to make his marriage commitment and blatantly reveled in his near-perfect results.

The outcome of my own questionnaire was in stark contrast from my future husband's. I not only wasn't inside the inner circle, I hadn't even made the outer circle. In fact, I was marked as a dot on the far edge of the page. Needless to say, I was not prepared for marriage, and our minister advised against our marrying at that time. But with rose-colored glasses and stubbornness on our side, Jamie and I ignored my comical but somewhat disturbing questionnaire results and continued forward with both our marital plans and the move away from my family.

Still, it wasn't until after the move that our different outlooks on marriage came to a head. As my marriage preparation test results suggested, I did bring a lot of idealism into our marriage, and my expectations were certainly out of touch with reality. But Jamie is the first to admit that he wasn't the easiest man to live with in those early years.

My need to depend entirely on my husband coupled with Jamie's need for independence created a growing disharmony in our union. Unfortunately, the more Jamie withdrew into his hobbies and work, the more insecure and needy I became. I was now a plane flight away from my family and friends, and I began to feel lonely. All of a sudden, the reality of *forever* hit me, and I began to resent being married. I also felt trapped, as though I was caught in a cocoon, wanting to fly but unable to move.

Then in mid-1996, I secured secretarial employment in nearby Melbourne, Victoria's capital city. My workplace interactions filled the void of loneliness I was experiencing at home. It also gave me new friendship circles apart from my husband.

But this newfound independence became the beginning of my own undoing. You see, I had by now learned to use my youthful beauty to my advantage. And through the various employment opportunities I was given, my pride got the better of me. The more admiration, compliments, and flattery I received, the more inflated my ego became and the less I sought such attention from my husband.

This inflated opinion of myself became even more pronounced when I began pursuing an acting career in film and television about a year or so after moving to Victoria. My new occupation coupled with various photographic modelling opportunities that came my way only fanned my need for approval. The more affirmation I received in each sphere of employment, secretarial as well as the film industry and modelling, the more self-centered I became, which further damaged our marriage.

Meanwhile, with me off living my own life puffed up in all the wrong ways, Jamie was sliding into depression. He experienced many melancholy days, which only exasperated his need to withdraw. This in turn made my running from our marriage seem justifiable to me.

To make matters worse, and perhaps contributing to the strain on our marriage, our faith beliefs were being rocked to the very core of who Jamie and I had always considered ourselves to be. This came about because the church sect in which both Jamie and I had been brought up was now declaring much of its teachings to be false. These teachings were based predominantly on Old Testament Mosaic Law. The denomination itself was a break-away of the Seventh Day Adventist church, and we observed Old Testament commandments religiously, keeping a variant of the seven Jewish holy days, which were Passover, the Feast of Unleavened Bread, Pentecost, Trumpets, Atonement, Feast of Tabernacles, and the Last Great Day.

We also kept the Sabbath from sundown Friday to sundown Saturday. This included refraining from any worldly activities. We went to church on Saturdays and believed worshipping on any other day disqualified you as a believer. We were told that we were the only saved church and that all other so-called Christians were wrong and unsaved.

Christmas, Easter, and birthdays were considered pagan, self-indulgent celebrations, so neither Jamie nor I had experienced any of these as children or into our early adulthood. Since we'd always been taught that these holidays had pagan origins, I also somehow attributed paganism to Jesus as well. It wasn't that I'd actually been taught this, but rather that it was a childhood misconception. Strangely, I did pray in Jesus's name to God the Father, who was very real to me even as a child. We also kept the Mosaic dietary laws, and we were taught that true believers were healed by faith in God and not through doctors.

The founder of our sect had also formulated an additional set of laws such as that women could not wear make-up and must only wear dresses or skirts to church. Men could not wear their hair long or wear earrings at any time. Laws such as those condemning interracial marriage as well marriage outside of church membership were enforced, while tithing up to 30% of income, depending on the year, was compulsory.

When you are involved in such a controlling organization as Jamie and I grew up in, you do not question what you are taught. The leaders make it very believable, and because everything is fear-based, you accept it lest you be disciplined or even excommunicated, which in turn would lead to being shunned by family and friends.

The church itself made its fellowship very exclusive and kept its flock well entertained. As a child, I never felt I was missing out because there were always camps, holidays, and other fun activities to enjoy inside the fold. While there were lots of rules and regulations, you obeyed these robotically, without question and with little or no pain.

Then in 1986, the founder of the denomination passed away, and all that Jamie and I had grown up knowing was declared false teaching by the new leader. New doctrines and teachings were announced, confusing sect members. By the time Jamie and I married in 1995, our world, our church, everything we'd ever known to be right and safe had come crashing down.

Eventually this included our marriage. Over those first couple of years, Jamie and I became less and less united. We fought often and started living quite separate and worldly lives. Our faith beliefs were unstable, our marital expectations were not aligning, and we didn't know what to believe any more. We had been fed a lie all our lives, and now we were both escaping, running, avoiding. Any whispers from God calling us back were squashed as we ran faster and faster towards earthly pleasures, evading the power of heavenly truth.

But amidst all this avoidance and despite the shakiness of our marriage, I was still clinging to my happily-ever-after childish fantasy. Somehow, I knew that although on the surface our union looked completely broken, Jamie and I were still in love, and I was certain that God even had a plan for our messy relationship.

So around 1997, two years after our wedding with our marriage on the rocks and our faith beliefs unhinged, Jamie and I entered phase two of my happily-ever-after plan. We began to get serious about having a baby. I say serious because in fact we had shown very little precaution during those first two years of marriage, so in all reality a pregnancy could have occurred at any time. But it was at this point that we consciously decided we were ready to be parents.

Initially, trying to conceive was fun and full of anticipation, and it brought us closer together. Like most couples embarking on this adventure, we would get giddy about what gender combination we would ideally love to have and the names we could call our offspring. We became "experts" on how to raise and not raise a child, and we expressed our own expectations of parenthood. We were excited about the next chapter of our lives, and as two young, healthy adults, we were surely only a moment's breath away from our dream becoming a reality.

But a year later, our quest to start a family was not looking good. Conception had not proved just a breath away. In fact, it was nowhere in sight! Phase two of my happily-ever-after was as much a failure as my marriage, and nothing was working out as I had imagined.

Instead of falling pregnant effortlessly, I found myself being challenged by God in my Christian walk. I was at a crossroads whereby my circumstances were drawing me back to the Father. My crumpled-up, confused belief system was being refined by my Creator, and it was through the very means by which God knew he could most gain my attention that he chose to speak to me.

Jamie and I remained childless for eight more years after our initial realization that something was wrong. We experienced terrible lows in our marriage during this time, and it was but by the grace of God that we persisted. To experience a yearning for so long takes its toll, and to go through such yearning separate from God nearly breaks you. But God is so faithful, and he meets you where you are at. He had a plan and purpose for our lives, and he was already starting that work in us.

God never abandoned me through my wilderness years. Instead he opened doors and guided me through to greener pastures, teaching and refining my faith and beliefs every step along the healing journey. Out of a painful barrenness state, God gained our attention and began a wonderful work in both Jamie and me.

My testimony is a story of God healing the whole person, not just the physical byproduct, which was the healing of my womb. Not only did I need healing from an empty, unfruitful womb, but I also needed many areas in my life to be touched by God. From personal healing to mending a belief system filled with legalism, untruths, and even misconceptions about Jesus himself, my journey through barrenness brought me freedom on countless levels and changed my life forever.

I have written *Having Faith* in three parts. In the first part, I continue my own story of coming out of legalism and into freedom through Christ. It was during this season that I learned that Jesus is all I need. And from that foundational perspective, I then began to hand over my will to his as I sought healing for my womb.

Building on my own story, I also in this section introduce three women of the Bible who had their own struggles with infertility. I look at the anguish of Sarah, Rachel, and Hannah, three of my favorite biblical characters, each desperate to become mothers and each with unique and special messages that are still relevant for us today. Through reading and studying their testimonies, my own faith increased, enabling me to continue seeking God's truth for my own barren womb.

The second part of this book goes deeper into my season of seeking. It was during this time that my faith was taken to higher grounds and my relationship with the Trinity of God became integral to my journey. Throughout this section, I will share some of the principles that helped me through my barrenness years, which I hope will encourage my readers to delve deeper into God's will for your own lives as well.

The third segment of this book is a testimony of God's faithfulness to his promise for my life. It is the end of my barrenness story and the beginning of my new life as a mum. While I was writing *Having Faith*, it was always my prayer that the words in this book would offer comfort and encouragement to its readers and that God would offer guidance through my testimony. I do not believe there is a single answer to receive healing from barrenness. I can only offer my testimony in hope that it will inspire others to seek God's truth for their own circumstances.

Just as each believer is called to *work out their own salvation* (Philippians 2:12), similarly the quest for freedom from infertility is a personal journey and unique to each situation. God deals with us all differently, therefore my testimony is distinctive to the healing I needed and not necessarily reflective on the walk that every other couple experiencing infertility will go on.

I started to write *Having Faith* in the early months of 2004 when I was still childless. I remained childless for two more Christmases. This greatly tested my faith, as my writing back then was only a projection of future things to come. I wrote from a state of belief and trust that what I was hearing from God would come to pass.

And God is so faithful. He guided me to a place of surrender that allowed him to work miracles in every area of my life that was damaged. From personal and matrimonial healing to spiritual rebuilding, God wrought restoration and spiritual victory in my life. And from there he granted a barren woman the desires of her heart—three beautiful children, a girl named Faith Crystal and two boys named Joel Samuel and Levi James.

It was out of a painful barrenness state that I came to find the truth about my Deliverer. In this wilderness time, my testimony was born. And through his truth and his faithfulness, Jesus became my Savior, my Redeemer, my Restorer, and my Healer. Although this is my story, it is Jesus's victory!

PART ONE:

Jesus Is All I Need

CHAPTER ONE:

New Foundation

"Therefore everyone who hears these words of mine and puts them into practice is like a wise man who built his house on the rock."

— Matthew 7:24

It was the year 2000 when I felt a strong yearning to begin attending a local Christian church. By this point three years had passed since Jamie and I first realized we had a problem with infertility. This was about the same amount of time since we'd left our previous church. That entire denomination was now going through a real crisis as it tried to deal with the new concept of grace superseding law.

Globally, members of this denomination were struggling to deal with the radical changes new leadership had introduced. Many ended up reverting to the legalistic, law-abiding, rule-making culture to which they'd grown accustomed. Others like Jamie and me had left that church angry, confused, and with our core beliefs and faith badly shaken.

In 2000, Jamie and I were still feeling lost and bemused, licking our wounds from our legalistic upbringing, struggling to keep our marriage afloat, and now dealing with the issue of my barren womb. And yet that was the moment when I took a rather large leap of faith. I had never attended a church outside the denomination in which I'd grown up, and the local church towards which I felt drawn seemed a far cry from what I was used to. Not only did it appear very modern and worldly, but its worship service was held on Sunday, a day I had always been told was not the true Sabbath. Not to mention I could hear loud, extremely contemporary music as I drove by, nothing like the sedate hymns I'd grown up singing.

Still, every Sunday on my way to the supermarket, I would drive past this church and feel a longing and curiosity to know more about it. By now I was in crisis mode with my life in ruins, and I was desperate for God in my life. I was living a double life, pretending my marriage and spiritual walk were on solid ground while the reality was just the opposite. I was a mess. My marriage was on the rocks. Childlessness had added to our marital woes. Worst of all, I didn't know what to believe spiritually any more.

So one Sunday morning, my heart thumping hard and nervous tension running through my body, I gingerly stepped foot into this local church. Jamie remained at home, outwardly skeptical of my decision, but I could tell he was inwardly intrigued. On this first visit, my plan was to sit quietly at the back of the church auditorium where no one would notice me. But God had other plans. An usher greeted me at the door and led me right to the front of the church.

The service was nothing like what I had experienced growing up. It was modern, upbeat, relevant, and it moved me like nothing before. It evoked praise and worship from my heart, something I had also never experienced before.

The focus of this church's worship was all about their Savior—Jesus—and his abundant love. We need do nothing to earn his love, but could come just as we are to Jesus. It was exactly the opposite of everything I'd ever been taught, and it was exactly everything I had ever needed.

At the end of the service, an altar call was offered, something I had never seen or heard of before. I think I may have had an out-of-body experience that day because somehow my legs carried me up to the front stage for prayer. I found myself standing there in front of a congregation I didn't know, tears streaming down my face, being prayed over by a pastor I'd never met while feeling completely loved and cared for by the only One who truly knew my deep pain and grief.

It felt as though God was personally reaching down to touch me, pulling me out of the wreckage that was my life and offering me a lifeline. By guiding me to this local church, God was positioning me to learn the truth about God's Son, Jesus, and to put away my childhood misconceptions as to his deity. In this place, a new foundation was beginning to take form.

Though my first visit to this church stirred my spirit as never before, it took another year before I had the courage to return. I think what kept me at bay was mostly a feeling of unworthiness and shame. I was also embarrassed by my outpouring of emotions that day, something completely foreign to me and which I did not realize was quite acceptable in other Christian cultures.

While the grip of fear and shame prevented my return, I learned later that an elder from this same church, Bob, took a train to work at the same station I did. He hadn't recognized me from my single visit to his church, but somehow he felt compelled by the Holy Spirit to pray for me every time he saw me boarding my train to go to work.

It was Bob's faithfulness to this prompting by God's Spirit, I truly believe, that in time enabled me to come *home*, as the Prodigal Son did, to my heavenly Father and family. Along with his wife Jan, Bob eventually became a close mentor and friend to Jamie and me, journeying closely with us in our quest for healing from barrenness.

Meanwhile, I was still driving past this church on Sunday mornings, watching, yearning for what they offered, but fearful of returning. It was early 2001 before I again mustered the courage to actually walk inside. And only my intense desire to experience again the closeness I'd felt with

God on my first visit impelled me to step once more out of my comfort zone. Once again, Jamie remained home, evaluating my choice from the sideline.

For a second time, the service moved me to tears, bringing me the closeness to my Creator I so desperately sought. And for a second time, my legs disobeyed me, carrying me to the front of the congregation for prayer. By now I was realizing this was something I'd have to get used in this season of my life.

From that moment on, I began regular attendance at church. In this space, I felt safe and loved. My heart would fill with hope as the music swept over me, bringing me a message of God's resounding love. The words being taught were grace-filled and life-giving. Teachings on who Jesus is and what he came to do on our behalf were restoring my brokenness. A lifetime of trying to please God through my own efforts was being replaced by simple faith. I now knew this was where I belonged.

Although increasingly intrigued, Jamie was battling his own misgivings towards any and all churches. So much so that even the thought of walking into a church brought on a panic attack. And so Jamie remained reluctant to join me.

For my part, as I became more involved with my new church, I began feeling a strong conviction that God wanted me to give up my employment in Melbourne to volunteer part-time as church administrator. Looking back, I can see this was God's strategic plan to remove me from the corporate scene, where my vanity was still being stroked, so that he could begin to transform me. But as you can imagine, my leaving a good, paying job to volunteer at a church didn't go down well with my husband.

Financially, we had just finished building a new house together in Sunbury, so a double income to pay off the mortgage would seem a much wiser choice. And though Jamie was open to my church attendance, he was still reluctant and skeptical towards churches in general. He was also afraid we would both get hurt all over again.

But as is his gentle and patient nature, Jamie accepted my decision to leave my paid work. So still in 2001, I took on the responsibility of church administrator. By God's grace, this soon became a paid position. I was still struggling with self-centeredness and a much-inflated ego, so along with working part-time at the church, I also embarked on a Bachelor of Arts degree, majoring in psychology and German. This only lasted a year, but was something I'd always wanted to do. I was also still pursuing an acting career in film and television, although my heart was increasingly unsettled with this choice of vocation.

By 2002, it became clear to me that my acting career did not fit with my Christian morals. Increasingly, I was being offered small but unwholesome acting jobs which I could not accept. In the end, this made giving up my acting an easy choice, especially since by now I had added to my administrative duties the role of director of the Church Welfare Centre, a role I remained in until our daughter was born in 2006.

Throughout 2001 and into 2002, I also began a journey of healing, both personally and from the religious cult system I had grown up in. This helped me recognize how self-indulgent and egotistic I had become. During this time period, I experienced a number of dreams in which Jesus revealed that he was all I needed. Over and over, Jesus reiterated that I didn't need to be affirmed by anyone else. I needed only to rely on him.

The love and acceptance I received from my Savior God made it an easy choice for me to lay all my earthly desires aside and to start following him alone. Through this perfect love that Jesus offered me, I began to heal as well from my selfishness. The more I healed the less external recognition I needed. This change in my heart greatly benefited my marriage. I started taking responsibility for things in my marriage that I needed to change. I also began to fervently pray for my husband and our union.

Can I just pause to say here what astounding results can come from a praying wife? Almost immediately, Jamie felt a desire to reestablish his relationship with God. Towards the end of 2001, despite some ongoing anxiety, my husband courageously re-entered a church for the first time since leaving our previous denomination. Within a short time, his attendance at church became the norm. Together we began a journey to restore our marriage and spiritual walk, building a new foundation for our lives on solid ground.

By the end of 2002, both our marriage and doctrinal beliefs were becoming more aligned with God's plan and purpose for our lives. We still had a long way to go and over the following two years would experience far more healing in our marriage as well as the emotional byproducts of our messy relationship and cultish upbringing. But we now felt ready at least to grow deeper in the faith and pursue healing for my womb.

Initially and rather naively I must say, I expected healing to come promptly once I'd emerged from legalism and begun understanding and experiencing freedom in Christ. Somehow, I'd assumed our legalistic upbringing was the only barrier preventing us from receiving the gift of parenthood. I had overlooked the instability in our own lives as well as in our marriage relationship, which also needed to mend.

What I've come to realize is that God wanted more for Jamie and me than simply becoming parents. He wanted to heal all of us, and since there were many layers that needed to be restored, this was going to take time.

The Old Testament book of Malachi speaks of a man and a woman becoming one in flesh and spirit:

> And why one? Because he [God] was seeking
> godly offspring. (Malachi 2:15)

This proved very true for Jamie and me. We needed our doctrinal beliefs restored and to become one in our marriage union before we could begin the process of producing godly offspring and raising them in the way of the Lord. This was part of God's restoration plan for our family.

So though our faith and marriage union were moving in the right direction, it was not yet God's timing for us to start a family. Then in 2004, our seventh year of wrestling with infertility and just shy of our ninth wedding anniversary, Bob and Jan, church elders and our faithful mentors, suggested we rededicate our marriage and Christian walk to God. Jamie and I agreed to hold an intimate ceremony with just this couple so we could confess our marital hurts audibly and recommit our wedding vows in front of witnesses.

That day Jamie and I invited Jesus to be at the helm of our union and our spiritual lives, and we have held him in that position ever since. We finalized the ceremony by joining with Bob and Jan in prayer and worship and partaking of the Eucharist together. As we shared the bread and wine, as we openly made and confessed new vows and declarations, Jamie and I were at last able to break ties once and for all with our former legalistic beliefs, restoring us as individuals and our marriage to what God intended for our lives.

Since that glorious ceremony, our marriage has gone from strength to strength all the way to the present day. It became a pivotal point in our life journey whereby our past was now history and we could allow our future to become his [God's] story.

From the time I began a new church experience in early 2001 to when we finally conceived our first child in late December, 2005, God was rebuilding our lives. Although during this season we experienced some of our loneliest and most challenging times, they were also among our most rewarding. For me personally, it was an intense, heartbreakingly honest season when God repeatedly gained my attention. Over those five years, Jamie and I received matrimonial and spiritual healing that led in turn to our physical restoration.

It may sound cliché to express being thankful for hardship when you come out the other end. But I am truly thankful for the nine years Jamie and I endured in the wilderness. Although every journey through infertility is unique and each couple should seek God for clarity in their own situation, I hope that my story can serve as a testimony of God's everlasting love and God's ability to remain faithful even when our faith is at its weakest.

I have come to realize that there is no special remedy or set of ingredients that releases physical healing bar one. Every situation requires its own touch from God, and he is the one immutable ingredient that must be present in any healing process. Jesus was the key to unlocking my womb from its barrenness state, and thus any victory and honor to be claimed in my story likewise belongs to him.

I have also come to believe that physical healing may be secondary to any essential spiritual healing. For Jamie and me, the curing of my womb was the byproduct of our spiritual and matrimonial restoration. It was the state of our heart, the condition of our spiritual lives, that first and foremost needed to be repaired.

Jamie and I had grown up in an exclusive religious group that conditioned our way of thinking and our way of living in such a way that we saw a relationship with God only through acts of service and obedience to the law. If we failed in those, we failed God.

This way of thinking had entwined itself into every area of our lives, so when our belief system disintegrated during those early marital years, it seemed easiest to abandon our faith altogether and run towards earthly pleasure as a substitute. Through our barrenness journey, we were released from this misconception, entering instead a new and liberating freedom that comes from the grace of Jesus Christ. In reestablishing a solid foundation for Jamie and me, God also restored our faith, our marriage, and then finally my womb.

I do not presume to understand every facet of why barrenness occurs. But I do hope that as I continue to share my testimony throughout this book, it will serve to inspire you to do as the writer of the New Testament letter to the Hebrews advises:

Run with perseverance the race marked out for you. (Hebrews 12:1)

CHAPTER TWO:

Faith is Born

"We do not want you to become lazy, but to imitate those who through faith and patience inherit what has been promised."

—Hebrews 6:12

When I was about six years of age, I went through a period where I had large warts over many parts of my hands. I remember feeling so embarrassed by their appearance, especially at school around the other children, that I began to pray to God that he would remove my warts.

The beliefs of our denomination forbade resorting to medical science for healing. Despite this, Mum and Dad took me to several doctors in an attempt to have these horrible growths removed. But due to their size and how they clumped together, nothing could be done medically to get rid of them. In light of this unfortunate circumstance, I decided to pray diligently on my own that God would heal me from this unsightly affliction. After four years of daily prayer, every single wart disappeared overnight.

I'm not sure why it took four long years before God intervened. Perhaps he was refining a young girl's perseverance. Or maybe it was to encourage my faith walk later in life. But there is something beautiful about the innocence of a child's faith. Regardless of the outcome, quite often a child will accept the result. There is purity in child-like faith that is difficult to find as adults. I think over the course of passing years we become trained to "get what we want when we want it", as the saying goes. So when we don't see instantaneous results, we equate this to unanswered prayer. This certainly proved true in my own case.

Nineteen years after this childhood faith encounter, sometime in 2002 shortly after Jamie and I had begun our rebuilding season, another tiny wart appeared on one of my fingers. Its arrival had a profound effect on me.

For years prior to this wart moment, Jamie and I had spent countless time and money seeking medical assistance for our infertility woes. In 1998, we began a thorough fertility workup to see if doctors could identify a cause for our infertility. Except for irregular menstrual cycles, everything seemed in good working order for both of us.

Over the next four years, Jamie and I completed numerous ovulation induction drug cycles, several intrauterine insemination (IUI) cycles, and two in-vitro fertilization (IVF) cycles, all procedures designed to increase opportunity for pregnancy. I also tried naturopathy to rebalance my reproductive system.

But medical assistance was not to be our answer. With each new procedure and every passing year, Jamie and

I became less optimistic about a positive result. In early 2002 after one final IVF cycle, Jamie and I came to the conclusion that medical help was not our solution. We both sensed that through our infertility God was drawing us back to himself. Neither Jamie nor I had stopped loving God even with the breakdown of our belief system and marriage. But both of us had been running, avoiding God's presence, and the use of medically-assisted fertility treatments was keeping us from drawing close to him.

So by the time this wart appeared in 2002, we had already gone through many years of medical treatments with no result and no real hope. As we grew spiritually, both Jamie and I began to understand that our situation was not a physical problem at all but rather a spiritual lock that needed to be opened. This spiritual truth, detailed in a later chapter, turned out to be a key factor to resolving our fertility struggles, although it took several years before this was confirmed and healing received.

We had also been given an unusual diagnosis at the conclusion of our last IVF cycle. The medical doctor involved described Jamie's sperm as incapable of penetrating into my eggs even though his sperm and my eggs were both adequately healthy. We were given the option to use a procedure called intracytoplasmic sperm injection (ICSI), a type of in-vitro fertilization that injects a sperm directly into a mature egg instead of the sperm doing this naturally on its own. The procedure had still not worked.

This diagnosis seemed to confirm our new spiritual awareness that our conception difficulties were caused by a spiritual blockage rather than a physical condition. This blockage, which we will also discuss later, would turn out to be one of many obstacles that needed to be overcome in order to bring about our deliverance.

So when I noticed this tiny wart on my finger, my heart was already being prepared to leave medical assistance behind and trust in God alone to answer my prayers for a baby. This wasn't an easy choice for me, and I was anxious about putting aside medically-assisted fertility treatments. But Jamie and I could both sense God drawing us near to him, and while we didn't yet have the answers, we both believed there was something more spiritual going on.

When I noticed the wart, I couldn't help but be reminded of the faith I'd once had as a child when I prayed daily for God to heal me from the warts all over my hands. This little wart was to me a memento of how in his timing God had answered a young girl's prayers. Astoundingly, my healing from infertility finally came about four years after this little wart appeared, the exact period of time it took for the warts on my hands to be healed in my childhood.

This tiny wart really did generate in me a new hope. It coincided with a timeframe where Jamie and I were on fire for God, pursuing him relentlessly (detailed in a later chapter). It stirred something deep within my heart, and somehow it enabled me to lay medical assistance aside and look to God alone for my healing.

Through the visual aid of this wart, I felt God was steering me on a new path, one that seemed to parallel the faith journey I had gone on as a child. It was at this pivotal point in time that the faith I once had a child was reborn and I decided to put my trust completely in the healing touch of God.

For over a year, this little wart remained on my finger as an emblem of the faith conviction Jamie and I held. But it wasn't always easy to remain faithful, especially when each passing year did not produce the outcome we were desperately seeking.

I found it so hard to trust God when our friends and family were having their own children with little or no effort while Jamie and I remained childless. Every time another couple announced their good news, my heart sank deeper and deeper until despair reigned. Time and time again, it seemed like a domino effect where everyone around was falling pregnant except for us. I tried to be happy for these others, but the reality of our own infertility felt too much for me to bear.

It was as though Jamie and I were caught in some time warp, standing still while friends and family progressed through the natural course of life. With each passing year, my heart continued to ache and yearn for what everyone else seemed to find so easy but was impossible for us. Living with the overwhelming pain and loss of childlessness while trying to believe for the miraculous healing of my womb was not easy. The appeal of further medical intervention was a constant temptation.

Many times during those first years of my faith journey from 2002-2004, I questioned whether God really heard or knew what we were going through. I wondered how long we would have to experience this pain while everyone around us received the blessings we longed for. Self-condemning thoughts spread havoc in my mind. I had moments where I told myself I didn't deserve the joy of motherhood. That perhaps I was being punished and God considered me unworthy to bear children.

Other times I wondered whether I had read too much import into a little wart. Maybe I should have continued on with medical assistance instead of believing in God for a miracle. Self-judgement reigned over me, and the loneliness and confusion I felt tested my ability to remain faithful.

But each time doubt tried to destabilize my faith, God would encourage me to stay the course. Through his Word, God aligned my thinking with his, and this strengthened my resolve. Jamie's strong conviction in the healing power of God also built up my faith.

Still, when I initially entered into this faith journey with God, my ability to trust remained the product of my legalistic church upbringing. I was approaching this faith appointment with a conditional heart. If I did something for God, like give up medical assistance and trust God to heal my womb, I should receive in return the reward of motherhood. I was making faith all about me, focusing on what I needed to accomplish in order to win the prize at the end.

Eventually, I would learn that faith is not about us at all. It's all about Jesus. I also came to realize that, along with this faith-by-works mentality, I had made an idol of my desire for motherhood. I was consumed with the worries and stresses of wanting to fall pregnant. Dependent on my need to actively seek a solution. Addicted to charting my course to ensure optimum opportunity for conception. It was, in fact, the opposite of faith and no different to when

I'd sought medical assistance outside of God's plan for my life.

This need to *do* something was a constant battle for me right throughout my infertility struggles. I remember attending a women's conference in 2005 where the speaker brought a message that spoke very clearly to me. In her message, she encouraged her audience to allow God to open the door for us and cease trying to do it all ourselves. This message had a powerful effect on me as I recognized that I was still inclined to *do* faith rather than *live by* faith, which is only achieved by focusing entirely on Jesus Christ.

The speaker's message also struck a chord because she was using the same pictorial representation of an open door for which I was desperately beseeching God. About a year earlier, I had received a prophetic vision of a door firmly closed over my womb. As I will share in a later chapter, that door turned out to be quite thick with many layers. So when the speaker spoke of open doors, my ears were already well inclined to pay attention.

Her message reminded me that conception was not going to happen by me trying to do it all on my own. Jesus was the key to unlocking the door, and no amount of charting my menstrual cycles for optimum conception was going to bring about my deliverance any faster. This was further confirmed to me when at the end of the service the speaker prayed this prophetic message over me: "Wait on the Lord. Cease being so consumed each month, even regimented, in trying to conceive. Trust in the Lord to do all that he desires."

God didn't want me consumed over my desire for children. He wanted me dependent on him, to let go of the reins and allow him to work accordingly in my life. This was faith in action.

It took me years to relinquish control. In reality, I think I toggled with this principle right through my infertility years. Certainly, the prophetic message I have just written about demonstrates that this was an ongoing struggle for me. But when I did submit myself to God and relinquish control, a peace and contentment came over me every single time.

God in his perfect patience and unconditional love remained steadfast and faithful. He always offered support and encouragement, especially when my faith was at its weakest. He showed me scriptures that aligned my thinking to believe in his divine intervention. He also brought people into both Jamie's and my life that stood firmly in faith, believing with us for our miracle.

And in his perfect timing, God intervened, unraveling his master plan for our lives little by little. It took over a year, at a time when I was finally ready if not always willing to surrender to my heavenly Father's will, before my little wart visual aid disappeared. It took a further three years before we received the blessing of parenthood.

As I've mentioned previously, healing needed to occur in the lives of both Jamie and me. Unlike miracles, healing usually takes time. Although Jesus paid the ultimate price for our healing and we did not have to earn that precious gift, within our own individual, matrimonial, and spiritual circumstances, restoration needed to take place.

With Jamie and me, God was realigning our lives with that of his will prior to the miracle of conception transpiring. I don't believe this means that God was withholding the gift of children from us, but rather providing a process in which healing could take place. Interestingly, the meanings of the names of our three children, which we received from God through prayer well before any of their births, reflect this healing course on which we were travelling. The names of our three children in the order the Holy Spirit gave them to us are Joel

Samuel, Levi James, and Faith Crystal. The meaning of their names is as follows:

- **Joel:** *God is willing.* **Samuel:** *God hears.*

- **Levi:** *two will be united as one.* **James:** *Supplanter.*

- **Faith** is self-explanatory, and **Crystal**, while actually meaning *a precious gem,* was given to me through a dream (mentioned later) depicting *healing.*

What I found astounding once I'd learned the meaning of our children's names was to see that through those names God had given Jamie and me a perfect one-line summary of our faith journey: "God is willing (and) he hears (and) the two will be united as one (by) the Supplanter (the One who supersedes and restores) (through) faith (and) healing."

Jamie and I were being restored in so many ways. Physical healing was taking place. Our marriage was being rebuilt on a firm foundation. Together as one, we were coming back to the heart of God. The meaning of our children's names reflects this beautifully. In our children, God left us a summation of our faith journey as a reminder of his amazing faithfulness!

It took an odd little visual aid on my finger back in 2002 to gain my attention and start me on a new journey of faith. Appearing on my finger nineteen years after my childhood faith experience, this little wart reminded me that nothing is impossible for God. It may take time for healing to occur, as was the case with both the healing of a six-year-old girl's warts and my nine years of barrenness. But God is faithful, and his timing is perfect.

Out of an ugly growth on my finger, a new faith was born in me. And because of the perfect faithfulness of our Lord and Savior Jesus Christ, another Faith was born four years later. Our daughter Faith, whose name embodies our

journey.

CHAPTER THREE:

My Faithful BibleCompanions

"The word became flesh and made his dwelling among us.

We have seen his glory, the glory of the one and only, who came

from the father, full of grace and truth."

– John 1:14

For much of my season of barrenness, I mostly felt like the Israelites, wandering the wilderness alone, lost and confused, never seeing the Promised Land and only having hope when God comforted and encouraged me along the way. Any optimism I felt was often short-lived as a fog of doubt and disbelief would eventually envelope me, clouding my judgment and ability to hear the message God intended for me to receive.

But God is merciful and faithful. Just as Joshua eventually led the Israelites into the Promised Land, so God fulfilled his promise in me by sending his son Jesus to lead the way. A psalm written by King David, often termed the Shepherd's Psalm, expresses it this way:

> The Lord is my shepherd, I shall not be in want. He makes me lie down in green pastures, he leads me beside quiet waters; he restores my soul. He guides me in paths of righteousness for his name's sake. (Psalm 23:1-3)

God guided me ever so gently to a place of humility and trust. But it was up to me to let go of my own strong will. In the Old Testament book of Proverbs, we are instructed:

> Trust in the Lord with all your heart and lean not on your own understanding; in all your ways

acknowledge him, and he will make your paths straight. (Proverbs 3:5-6)

Though a slow learner, I eventually came to understand this. I ceased leaning on my own limited knowledge, and I started to find rest in my Savior. Then in early 2004, a few months prior to our marriage rededication ceremony, I decided it was time to learn what truths God's Word held about barrenness. For over a year when I had a free day from work, I researched words and phrases in the Bible that confirmed God's intent for humanity to conceive and bear children. These Bible verses, which I have included in Appendix II, greatly encouraged me and enabled me to continue trusting God for what seemed an impossibility.

The Holy Spirit also led me on a study of six women in the Bible who were also barren. My research showed me that each of these women's barrenness only lasted for a season, and each woman eventually received the blessing of children. This greatly heartened me. I am not saying these biblical stories offer a guarantee of being healed from infertility. Jesus is our Healer, and therefore any healing is at his discretion.

But what did encourage me in these six women's testimonies was the underlying message resounding throughout their stories that God is in control. Their inability to conceive when they wanted was not a punishment from God. Nor was it because these women were not favored by God. In fact, quite the opposite was true. Rather, it was because they were each part of a giant jigsaw puzzle called the perfect plan of God.

Over the next three chapters, I will deviate somewhat from my own testimony to share the stories of three of these six women the Bible references as being barren. I am focusing mainly on Sarah, Rachel, and Hannah as they are the three women I felt led to write about during my time of research in 2004. But I have also included in the appendixes biblical references of the other three barren women.

The infertility struggles of Sarah, Rachel, and Hannah each illustrate in a different way that God was in control of their lives. Many times I found myself questioning whether God knew or even cared about what Jamie and I were going through. Barrenness is such a lonely journey that it often left me feeling abandoned. The message presented in the testimonies of Sarah, Rachel, and Hannah demonstrates that God not only knows and cares, but is intricately involved in each of our lives.

I have chosen to place these testimonies in this section of the book because it was through these three women's faith journeys that my own faith increased and that I began a new season of discovery, which I write about in succeeding chapters. As I examined the brief sketch Scripture gives us of their lives and how they endured the barrenness experience, I was encouraged to continue pursuing God for the healing of my own womb.

Sarah is the first woman of faith I write about. Her testimony offers us an example of patience, perseverance, and waiting for God's perfect will. The biblical account also demonstrates that there are consequences when we choose to act separately from God's will. This doesn't mean necessarily that those consequences are God's direct punishment for stepping outside his will. Rather, because God's will is perfect, anything outside his will is not. But as Sarah's story also demonstrates, God doesn't need perfection from us in order for his purpose to unfold. God can turn our poor choices around and still make them apart of his overall plan for our lives.

Rachel's barrenness journey reveals more of the beauty behind the jigsaw puzzle that is God's design for each of our lives. Her story demonstrates that God has a purpose for each and every one of us and that our circumstances may be part of a bigger picture. In Rachel's case, her infertility was an intentional segment of God's plan, incorporating her sister Leah into God's design. In this story, we see some of the more unconventional ways in which God may choose to work.

Hannah's testimony, I believe, represents the true heart of a barren woman. In response to a heartfelt, desperate prayer, God listened, found favor, and fulfilled Hannah's deep yearning for a child. Hannah's story also reveals that sometimes a game-changer moment is required in order for transformation to occur. And here again, as was the case in all three women's barrenness journeys, we can see God behind the scene, orchestrating a triumphant ending to Hannah's painful circumstances.

Sarah, Rachel, and Hannah all encountered similar heartache, an anguish that still exists today within the hearts of those who are barren. These three women lived under the old Jewish covenant, which required obedience to the

Mosaic laws and during which time there was not the same direct access to our heavenly Father we now have as believers under the covenant of Jesus Christ (Romans 8:26-27, 34; Hebrews 4:14-16). Still, all three women's stories make abundantly clear that each of their journeys was unique and very personal to God.

That has not changed. In fact, for those who believe Jesus is their Lord and Savior, access to our Father in heaven becomes very real and personable. Jesus has become our new covenant, paying the ultimate penalty for our lives when he died on the cross and was raised from the dead over two thousand years ago. He accomplished his purpose here on earth, which was to bring salvation, healing, restoration, and offer himself as a blood sacrifice so that we could not only have an intimate relationship with God, but also receive the blessings our wonderful Father desires to offer us.

There are numerous encouraging passages in the Bible that confirm God's desire to bless us and make us fruitful. As mentioned before, I've included some of these at the back of the book. Some may call these scriptures promises and the rightful inheritance of every Christian. Others may feel differently and have their own life story to suggest otherwise. What you glean from God's inspiring words is between you and your Creator.

But whatever our personal conviction on this, we can agree that Jesus should always be our main focus. It is on Jesus that our eyes should be fixed (Hebrews 12:2) and to Jesus that our delight and worship should be directed, regardless of the outcome.

For many years I had a works mentality, believing that if I spoke out often enough the promises God offers in the Bible and prayed and meditated on them on a regular basis, I would receive what I had asked for. Although I believe we indeed should confess aloud God's Word and embed it into our hearts, my approach in striving constantly to effect a particular outcome only left me confused and downcast when no such result materialized.

What I came to realize was that when I *did* faith rather than lived by faith, which is achieved only through focusing on and delighting in the Savior, I was engaging in an unending battle of the mind, never knowing whether I had done enough to win the prize at the end. Isaiah 64:6 tells us that "all our best efforts are but filthy rags before the Lord." This means that no amount of *doing* will accomplish God's work. I finally learned that all God required of me was to trust him. From there, I could be open to receive all Jesus had in store for me.

The following three chapters devoted to Sarah, Rachel, and Hannah give a summary of their biblical narratives along with an interpretation I believe God placed on my heart to share with you. As stated before, I have included these testimonies as a reminder of God's sovereignty and faithfulness towards his people as well as to encourage us to stand firm in believing and trusting our heavenly Father.

Each of these women shows a real human side of the pain and anguish of infertility. They are examples of the choices we sometimes make in desperate situations. They represent the loneliness of bearing this burden. They also typify the hostile environment a barren woman may face. Sarah, Rachel, and Hannah are sometimes courageous and sometimes faithful, but they are also sometimes weak and stoop to grabbing for earthly solutions.

In other words, they are women just like you and me!

After their stories, I will continue on with my own testimony and share the rest of my season of discovery. But for now, may these next three chapters devoted to our biblical counterparts bless you and reveal to you God's perfect plan for our lives that is evident in their testimonies.

CHAPTER FOUR:

Mother of Nations

*"Those who believe are children of Abraham . . . So those who
have faith are blessed along with Abraham, the man of faith. Christ
redeemed us . . . in order that the blessing given to Abraham might
come to the Gentiles through Christ Jesus, so that by faith we might
receive the promise of the Spirit." — Galatians 3:7, 9, 13-14*

"**M**other of Nations" was the prophetic endearment God gave to childless ninety-year-old Sarai when he changed her name to Sarah. God changed her husband Abram's name to Abraham during this same conversation, signifying "Father of Many Nations". God went on to tell Abraham about his wife:

I will bless her and will surely give you a son by her. I will bless her so that she will be the mother of nations; kings of peoples will come from her . . . Your wife Sarah will bear you a son, and you will call him Isaac. I will establish my covenant with him as an everlasting covenant for his descendants after him . . . My covenant I will establish with Isaac, whom Sarah will bear to you by this time next year. (Genesis 17:16, 19, 21)

To understand the significance of this prophetic word, we need to go back to when it all started for Sarah and Abraham. In fact, their barrenness story really began many decades prior to this prophecy coming to fruition.

Sarah was barren when she first married Abraham (Genesis 11:30). The Bible doesn't tell us at what age the couple married. But we do know they left their own country where their extended family lived when Abraham was seventy-five and Sarah ten years younger (Genesis 12).

When God spoke to Abraham in the above conversation, Sarah was eighty-nine years of age, Abraham almost a hundred. So for at least the twenty-five years since the couple left their homeland, the Bible makes reference to Sarah's barren condition.

Throughout this season of continued infertility, Abraham received a number of prophetic visions from God detailing the blessed future Abraham would lead. One such prophecy came at a time when Abraham was not feeling all that blessed. In fact, he was deeply troubled about his childless circumstances. He and Sarah had been barren for decades by this point, and he had become worried that since he had no children a servant in his household would become his heir, as was their cultural practice. But the Lord encouraged Abraham, telling him:

> Do not be afraid, Abram. I am your shield, your
> very great reward . . . This man will not be your

heir, but a son coming from your own body will

be your heir. (Genesis 15:1 -4)

This prophetic word included no timeframe as to when Abraham's heir would be conceived, but was given to offer Abraham and Sarah hope and encouragement as they waited expectantly for their moment of deliverance. I can imagine Sarah's excitement when her husband related God's revelation to her. I expect they both held on to the hope they had received for as long as possible. I certainly remember various prophetic revelations Jamie and I received, which I will tell you about later, that strengthened our resolve and helped keep us focused.

But time can wear the best of us down. As the years continued to pass by and the prophecy remained unfulfilled, Abraham and Sarah began to question the word from God Abraham had received. Sarah especially began to doubt the conviction they had both held on to for so long. It was in the midst of this uncertainty that they came up with what seemed a possible loophole in the prophecy. After all, God hadn't said at this point that Abraham's heir would come through Sarah. So instead of waiting on God's deliverance, Sarah presented an alternate strategy to her husband:

> The Lord has kept me from having children. Go,
> sleep with my slave [Hagar]; perhaps I can build
> a family through her. (Genesis 16:2)

Clearly doubt had already established its reign over both their lives for Sarah to present this idea to Abraham. I recognize the yearning to procreate that must have been close to the surface for both of them. It was certainly all-consuming for Jamie and me.

I also can't help but think the reasoning game that led to Sarah's change of plan had started a long time before their actions caught up. I can almost see the rational take form. God hadn't actually said that Abraham's heir would come from Sarah. In their culture, it was an acceptable custom for a man to take one of his wife's maidservants for the purpose of securing a male successor. In fact, both wives of Abraham's grandson Jacob did this, as we will see later in Rachel's story (Genesis 30), resulting in several of the twelve tribes of Israel.

So maybe logic suggested to Abraham and Sarah that it was time to stand up, be an adult, and do something about their problem. After all, God could heal Sarah's womb, but he hadn't done so. They had an unfulfilled prophecy that needed to be fulfilled. Neither Abraham nor Sarah were getting any younger. And here was a perfectly good alternative available in Hagar.

Yes, I can empathize with their desperation and see justification clouding their judgment. So as the story continues, a now timeworn and probably pressured Abraham agreed to Sarah's plan, took Hagar as his concubine, and Hagar conceived (Genesis 16:2-3).

I'm not sure what equivalent scenario we might have in our culture today that would come close to

Abraham and Sarah's choice. Perhaps the closest comparison might be a surrogacy plan that goes horribly wrong. But I think their story is not so much what Abraham and Sarah chose to do, but rather the consequence of doing it outside God's plan and purpose for their lives. That, I think, is very relatable for us today.

You see, from the moment Hagar became the surrogate mother, which was not in God's will, the dynamics of Abraham and Sarah's household changed significantly. Where harmony once reigned, there was now a hostile environment with two women at war and a husband stuck in the middle of their conflict. Scripture tells us how difficult life got in their home:

> When Hagar knew she was pregnant, she began
> to despise her mistress. Sarai blamed Abram
> saying, "You are responsible for the wrong I am
> suffering. I put my slave in your arms, and now
> that she knows she is pregnant, she despises me.

May the Lord judge between you and me."

(Genesis 16:4-5)

Going counter to God's plan for their lives made for a very unhappy household. Similarly, when I chose to pursue medical assistance, a choice that was not in accordance with God's plan for Jamie and me, my life also got messy. I spent years going around and around in circles, confused, weary, and downcast. All my self-pursuit did was bring me right back to where I started and where God was waiting for me to follow the right path instead.

In Sarah's story, her choice to go counter to God's will hurt their household deeply. Not a single person in this triangle of pain remained unaffected by Sarah and Abraham's decision. On the one hand you have Sarah, initiator of this surrogacy proposal, so desperate for a child she was blind to any grief her choice might bring to their household or how this act of surrogacy might turn out.

Then there's poor Hagar, used by her masters to get what they want. Unable to refuse, but unwilling to surrender, Hagar must have felt completely exploited by the people she served. As for Abraham, he is so disgruntled with the whole thing that he wipes his hands of his responsibility towards Hagar:

> Your slave is in your hands," Abram said. "Do with her whatever you think best." Then Sarai mistreated Hagar; so she fled from her. (Genesis 16:6)

Hagar, the innocent party in all of this, feels the injustice heaped upon her. Just because of her position as a slave, Hagar is used, mistreated, and trapped into a situation not of her choosing. So she runs away from her responsibilities as a servant of Abraham's household.

It is really hard to blame Hagar for escaping Sarah's wrath, especially by the standards of today's culture. But as a slave, her duty remained with her mistress regardless of any ill-treatment. It was near a water spring in the desert that Hagar finds reason and is able to find the strength to return home. There she is met by an Angel of the Lord:

> Then the angel of the LORD told her, "Go back to your mistress and submit to her." The angel added, "I will increase your descendants so much that they will be too numerous to count." The angel of the Lord also said to her: "You are now with child and you will have a son. You shall name him Ishmael, for the Lord has heard of your misery. He will be a wild donkey of a man; his hand will be against everyone and everyone's hand against him, and he will live in hostility toward all his brothers." (Genesis 16:9-12)

Although this word the angel delivered to Hagar had some ugly truths about the life her son would lead, it was exactly what she needed to turn her around. Hagar was clearly very distressed when the angel of the Lord found her, and just his presence there made her feel worthy and valued again. Hagar returned home feeling loved and worthy again, and a few months later the angel's message was fulfilled:

> So Hagar bore Abram a son, and Abram gave the name Ishmael to the son she had borne. Abram was eighty-six years old when Hagar bore him Ishmael. (Genesis 16:15)

Hagar's part in all of this is really significant to us. She was a slave, in bondage, a servant to her mistress. She was never free to make her own choice in any of this, and the birth of her son was evidence of her position of slavery.

In this story, Hagar represents the old covenant— laws, restrictions, bondage. All things with which I am very familiar. In his epistle to the Galatians, the apostle Paul draws a parallel between Hagar's position and the bondage we experience if we insist on living under the old covenant of rules and regulations given to Moses on Mount Sinai:

Tell me, you who want to be under the law, are you not aware of what the law says? For it is written that Abraham had two sons, one by the slave woman and the other by the free woman. His son by the slave woman was born according to the flesh, but his son by the free woman was born as the result of a divine promise. These things are being taken figuratively: the women represent two covenants. One covenant is from Mount Sinai and bears children who are to be slaves: this is Hagar. Now Hagar stands for Mount Sinai in Arabia and corresponds to the present city of Jerusalem, because she is in slavery with her children. But the Jerusalem that is above is free, and she is our mother. (Galatians 4:21-26)

For the believer today, this mirrors a life void of the freedom that comes through our Lord Jesus Christ, who is the new covenant that fulfills the old. In Sarah's story, this freedom is symbolized by the eventual birth of Abraham's and Sarah's own son, Isaac, born from a promise of God. But it would take thirteen more years before Abraham and Sarah would receive this promise. I can imagine how difficult those years must have been for Sarah. She must have felt so overwhelmed when Hagar returned home to have her baby. Maybe she even hoped Hagar would disappear permanently. It must have been heartbreaking for Sarah to watch her husband raise a son who was not her own.

For Jamie and me, I know watching our family and friends procreating took its toll. What should have been the happiest of occasions to participate in became painfully sad for us. It's not to say we resented our friends and family bearing children. We saw it as the most beautiful gift any couple could receive, and we were thrilled for our nearest and dearest. But their joy made us sorely aware of what we desperately wanted for ourselves but had come to seem nearly impossible.

Similarly, Sarah must have felt very alone in bearing this burden alone as she watched another woman raising her husband's son, an experience she'd expected to be part of her own destiny. With her own biological clock counting down, those thirteen years Sarah endured watching Hagar's son taking center stage in her husband's eyes must have been unbearable.

But God is ever gracious, and he fulfills his plan for each of our lives in his perfect timing and even when we stray way off course.

It is at this point in the story that we return to the prophecy we discussed at the beginning of this chapter, where God renamed the main cast to Sarah and Abraham, designating them as mother and father of all nations. This was Sarah's redeeming hour, a moment I can well relate to. She, a barren woman now well past the childbearing age, was not only given a name describing her as a fruitful mother to all, but the same prophecy proclaimed her upcoming pregnancy, a miracle beyond all physical possibilities.

Sarah was ninety years of age and had already entered menopause when she conceived and bore her son Isaac. Since their life spans were longer (Sarah died at a young 127 years while Abraham lived to a ripe old age of 175; see Genesis 23:1; 25:7), Sarah's age would be similar to a barren and menopausal woman today conceiving in her late 40s or 50s. A scenario that would require the miraculous. But this physical barrier did not prevent God from being able to perform a miracle in Sarah's life. No medical diagnosis nor age barrier is too difficult for God to intervene and prevail. Sarah is proof of this, and her story can surely encourage us today.

Isaac's birth to Sarah was the fulfillment of a promise made by God, given originally to Abraham well before Sarah's surrogacy plan was ever devised. This is important to note. Isaac's birth was the perfect will of God for Abraham and Sarah, and God had made that evident in his prophecy to Abraham. It was Sarah and Abraham who went outside that plan by incorporating their maidservant into the picture.

Likewise, when Jamie and I followed our own path rather than pursue what God's will was for us, we experienced a tumultuous ride. There is no substitute for God's plan for our lives. After all, it is perfect!

As we read above (Galatians 4:21-26), the apostle Paul explains to the Galatians that the two births in Sarah's and Abraham's story represent two separate covenants. This is relevant to us today. Ishmael's birth to Hagar was the result of her position of slavery, and it was not part of the promise of God. Meanwhile Isaac's birth was symbolic of that promise, and it represents the freedom that comes through Jesus Christ.

Jesus fulfilled the old covenant by offering us his grace and his righteousness. Whereas the old covenant has a "me" focus (what am I doing wrong to not receive the gift of motherhood, and how can I change my circumstances), the new covenant focuses entirely on Jesus and everything he has done right for us. As born-again believers living under the new covenant, we have freedom to rest in Jesus. Freedom to not be troubled by our circumstances as the apostle Paul goes on to say:

> It is for freedom that Christ has set us free. Stand firm, then, and do not let yourselves be burdened again by a yoke of slavery. (Galatians 5:1)

Jesus came to redeem us from the yoke of slavery, which is the law (Galatians 3:13), and therefore:

> If you belong to Christ, then you are Abraham's seed, and heirs according to the promise (Galatians 3:29)

This scripture means that all believers in Christ share in the inheritance alongside the Father of Nations, Abraham, because of our Lord and Savior's redemption.

Although Abraham's and Sarah's poor judgment cost their household dearly and complicated their lives, God always had a perfect plan for them. It was always in his design to bless their union with a child born from a promise. Through free will, God allows us to make our own choices, right or wrong. But just as Sarah discovered, as did also in time Jamie and me, God has a perfect will for each of our lives, and the blessings we can experience by pursuing God in our situation are comparable to none.

Like Sarah, I spent way too many years living counter to God's will for my life. While trying to avoid God, especially early in our marriage when Jamie's and my belief system was so mixed-up, I pursued parenthood my own way. I was in a very selfish place, so I felt it my right to engage in whatever medical practices were available in order to ultimately win the prize. But that was not God's perfect plan for our lives. God wanted to do something different for Jamie and me, something grander than my simplistic design.

Just as God was orchestrating a scenario whereby Sarah and Abraham would be redeemed into a mother and father of all nations, God was restoring all of my brokenness as well. Although I saw conception as the ultimate reward, God wanted to heal all of me, and that resulted in a much greater gift than I could have ever imagined.

Abraham and Sarah had to wait many decades for their miracle, Jamie and I almost a decade. But no matter how long it takes, no matter what your physical circumstances are, you are in God's design, and he has a beautiful plan and purpose for each one of our lives.

CHAPTER FIVE:

An Unconventional God

"For my thoughts are not your thoughts, neither are your ways my ways, declares the Lord!" —Isaiah 55:8

Isaac, the promised son of Abraham and Sarah, married Rebekah when he was forty years of age. Like her mother in-law Sarah, Rebekah was barren. But Isaac prayed to God on her behalf, and she became pregnant with twin boys, whom they named Jacob and Esau (Genesis 25).

Jacob and Esau had quite a volatile relationship even within their mother's womb, where they jostled one another (25:22). The firstborn of the twins, Esau, was a rugged, hairy man, skillful at hunting. As the firstborn, he would expect to inherit the birthright, i.e., the same blessings offered by God to his grandfather Abraham and then to his own father.

The second twin, Jacob, was Esau's complete opposite. He was a quiet man, less hairy, who preferred to stay among the tents. He was also more favored by his mother Rebekah (Genesis 25:19-28). Unlike Esau, who eventually despised his birthright (Genesis 25:34), Jacob understood, valued, and coveted the inheritance of a blessing from God belonging to the firstborn.

The time came when Isaac summoned Esau to receive from him the blessing that was part of his inheritance as firstborn. By this point, Isaac was about a hundred years old and almost blind. Rebekah, who favored Jacob over Esau, conspired a plan to ensure that her husband's blessing went to Jacob instead. Knowing her husband could not see the twins, Rebekah clothed Jacob in Esau's finest set of clothing, which carried Esau's unique odor (no deodorant back then!), then covered his hands and neck with goatskin so he would feel hairy like his brother. She sent Jacob to Isaac, who was deceived and pronounced over Jacob the blessing that by birthright should have gone to Esau as firstborn (Genesis 27).

Although Esau had so little interest in his father's blessing he'd actually sold it to his brother in return for a quick meal (Genesis 25:27-34), he was furious with his brother for stealing it from him. Esau planned to murder his twin, which forced his parents to send Jacob away for his own safety. They also commissioned Jacob to take a wife from among the daughters of Laban, Rebekah's brother (Genesis 28:1-2). Ironically, it would be through his uncle Laban that Jacob would find himself on the other end of betrayal and receive payback for the way he had deceived his twin.

The trickery that happens in this story is a typical characteristic of Satan, the thief of the world. Satan loves nothing more than to rob and steal our birthright while convincing God's children that they are barren and will remain that way always. Satan's character is the complete opposite of our loving Father.

Unlike Jacob, and indeed Satan, our heavenly Father does not steal or withhold blessing from us. Although it took nine years for Jamie and me to bear children, I am confident that God was not withholding the gift of children from us, but rather restoring that which was broken in order to bring about our deliverance. I do, however, accept that God's thoughts are not our thoughts, nor are our ways God's ways, as Scripture makes clear:

> "For my thoughts are not your thoughts, neither are your ways my ways," declares the Lord. "As the heavens are higher than the earth, so are my ways higher than your ways and my thoughts than your thoughts." (Isaiah 55:8-9)

God can and does increase blessing even when what we are asking for is not what we receive. I think the remainder of this story demonstrates well God's unconventional ways. It shows us that we cannot put God's ways in a box. He is too big for that. It also demonstrates that God's plans are always perfect, even if they end up being very different from our own expectations.

It was amongst Laban's household that Jacob met the love of his life. Laban had two daughters, the eldest named Leah and the younger Rachel. Leah was not considered particularly attractive, whereas Rachel is described as being lovely in form and very beautiful. Jacob fell in love with Rachel, so he asked Laban for her hand in marriage in return for seven years of labor (Genesis 29:16-18).

Laban accepted these terms, and after working for seven years, Jacob was granted marriage to Rachel, whom he loved. But during the wedding feast, Laban tricked Jacob into marrying his eldest daughter Leah by sending her to the marriage bed instead of Rachel (Genesis 29:22).

When Jacob woke up the next morning and recognized that he'd been deceived, he became angry. After a heated exchange, Laban agreed to let Jacob marry Rachel, but only upon the completion of the bridal week with Leah and in return for another seven years of labor (Genesis 29: 25-27).

What a masterful betrayal and lesson for Jacob on how his own trickery towards Esau must have made his brother feel! Jacob had already completed seven years of hard work as the marriage price for his beloved Rachel. Now on top of being scammed into an unwanted marriage with Leah, he had to complete another seven years of labor in order to marry the woman he had always loved and for whom he already had worked so hard and long.

To his credit, Jacob did as his father-in-law requested. Once Leah's bridal week was over, Jacob finally married his sweetheart, then went on to work another seven years for Laban as promised. But now a new problem is added to this twisted story of betrayal among siblings. Jacob loved Rachel more than Leah, so a new rivalry between siblings began.

It is at this point of the story where we see God's unconventional ways take form. God not only seems to assist Leah in her unloved state, but through her sets up a lineage that is essential to his plans for mankind. As the unloved wife, Leah was shown mercy by the Lord, who opened her womb. Leah gives birth to one son after another while Rachel remains barren (Genesis 29:31-35).

While I don't have a sister, I can relate to both Leah's and Rachel's circumstances. I think anyone going through a journey of barrenness has experienced having family members and friends procreate while you are not. It is painful and not just for the barren couple. Knowing how hurtful it can be for someone going through infertility, those who get pregnant sometimes find it hard to share their good news with infertile friends. The difference in circumstance can challenge a friendship.

It was even worse for Leah and Rachel since they also shared the same husband. Both sisters had something to offer their husband, but neither were happy. Leah desperately wanted to be loved by Jacob, which can be seen in the names she gives her first three sons:

> Leah became pregnant and gave birth to a son. She named him Reuben, for she said, "It is because the Lord has seen my misery. Surely my husband will love me now." She conceived again, and when she gave birth to a son she said, "Because the Lord heard that I am not loved, he gave me this one too." So she named him Simeon. Again she conceived, and when she gave birth to a son she said, "Now at last my husband will become attached to me, because I have borne him three sons." So he was named Levi. (Genesis 29:32-34)

These names Leah chose reflected the state of her heart. She was obviously very much aggrieved and felt deeply her husband's lack of affection. The trickery of forcing Jacob into marriage with Laban's eldest daughter had resulted in a profoundly unhappy marriage for Leah. It also created an enormous rift between the two sisters.

Rachel's circumstances were very different from Leah's. Unlike her sister, Rachel received fully her husband's affections. She was the favored wife, the woman whom Jacob had always loved. But like her sister, Rachel was unhappy. She was desperate for a baby. As she witnessed Leah's joy at bearing Jacob sons, Rachel began to feel jealous.

I know what jealousy feels like. It is a poisonous emotion that results in covetousness and resentfulness. At times during my barren years, jealousy would bubble away under the surface ready to explode. Jealousy prevented me from being genuinely happy for someone else's good fortune, and it made me resentful towards my Creator.

But God in his mysterious ways always knows what he is doing. The Old Testament patriarch Job, who experienced firsthand how mysterious God's ways can be, wrote:

Can you fathom the mysteries of God? Can you

probe the limits of the Almighty? (Job 11:7).

And while neither Rachel nor Jamie and me could fathom what God was doing in our lives, God had a very clear picture in mind. In Rachel's circumstances, God had an overall blueprint in hand for the nation of Israel. In our situation, God was restoring first our own brokenness.

Rachel was hurting, and I have no doubt God heard and felt her sorrowful cries. But behind the scene beyond what Rachel could witness, God was designing a master plan that included Leah being mother to half of Jacob's twelve sons, including Levi, ancestor to the Aaronic priestly line, and Judah, ancestor of King David as well as ultimately our Savior Jesus Christ. Had Rachel been fertile from the beginning, perhaps the twelve tribes of Israel would never have come into being. Leah was, after all, the unloved wife and Rachel Jacob's one true love. Perhaps Rachel's barrenness was essential to God's plan and the birth ultimately of six of Jacob's sons.

Rachel's story demonstrates that God's handiwork is not always recognizable during the event. The larger picture shows that Rachel's barrenness was part of a bigger God-plan. God was establishing a course for generations to come, including the bloodline through which would be born his Son, Jesus Christ.

It's not always easy to identify with God's vision and purpose for our lives. Sometimes what we think we need or want is not what God has planned for us at the time. Sometimes, as illustrated in Rachel's and Leah's story, God is working on something greater than we might expect. I know that proved true for Jamie and me. Had Jamie and I conceived immediately, perhaps our complete restoration would not have been forthcoming. After all, it was infertility that started us on a healing journey in the first place.

As human beings, we only see things from an earthly perspective. But God sees things fully and infinitely. God is in control, and no matter how long it takes, how hard it gets, we must have faith that God is preparing the way.

It was only after the birth of Leah's six sons and a daughter plus two sons each to Leah's and Rachel's maidservants, whom like Hagar, they had presented to their husband to bear children for them (Genesis 30:1-12), that God eventually remembered Rachel:

> Then God remembered Rachel; he listened to her
> and enabled her to conceive. She became
> pregnant and gave birth to a son and said, "God
> has taken away my disgrace." She named him

Joseph, and said, "May the Lord add to me another son." (Genesis 30:22-24)

God answered Rachel's request for a second son, and she bore Jacob his twelfth son Benjamin just before she died. God has a plan and purpose for each of our lives as well, and he is longing to chart it right now. We were created to be loved by God, not to live a life of disharmony without him. Scripture tells us that God wove together our very being and knew in advance every day of our lives before we were ever born:

> For you created my inmost being; you knit me together in my mother's womb . . . My frame was not hidden from you when I was made in the secret place, when I was woven together in the depths of the earth. Your eyes saw my unformed body; all the days ordained for me were written in your book before one of them came to be. (Psalm 139: 13-16)

Just as God knit us together in our mother's womb, so too does he have a perfect design sketched for our existence. Rachel's story shows us that there is more at work than perhaps is visible. We can't always see or hear what God is preparing for us. But be assured he planned you since before you were born and has your best interest at heart.

There were many times when I couldn't see clearly the path set out before me. It was so challenging and lonely, and sometimes I had no sense of God's footsteps nearby at all. But that doesn't mean he wasn't walking beside me all along.

Likewise, Rachel and Leah may not have felt that God was in control of their lives, but hindsight shows us that God was working tirelessly on their behalf, intervening in both of their lives. For Leah, God filled the void of love and adoration missing in her marriage to Jacob through the birth of her children. Conversely, Rachel already had her husband's affection. What Rachel desperately sought was a baby. This God granted her twice at his own appointed and perfect time.

Jacob's twelve sons went on to become the tribes of Israel, used by God to affect the course of history. Prophets, priests, and kings came from these twelve tribes of Israel as did ultimately the King of all mankind, the Messiah, Jesus Christ.

We don't know nor can we always see everything that goes on behind the scene. Just like watching a theatre production, we only see the performing cast up on stage. We are not privy to what goes on backstage. God is like the production director and crew in the wings, and when we invite him to take control; he works tirelessly on our behalf. Although it is sometimes easier in retrospect to recognize God's handprint on a situation, I hope that Rachel's and Leah's story, and indeed my own, can serve as a testimony of God's faithfulness and tender loving care for his children. God's background nudging guided me continuously to a place of surrender and submission. From there he continued to help me to stay the course over the last few years of my journey. There were many times when I didn't recognize God's part in my journey. But reflecting back now, I can definitely see his stamp all over it.

This was true for Leah and Rachel too. God cared for Leah, the unwanted wife, by filling her home with the love of children. He also showed mercy on Rachel, blessing her with two sons of her own. God took a very messy situation that began with betrayal and trickery and turned it completely around, bringing about amazing results. A lineage of prophets, priest, and kings resulted from the births of Rachel's and Leah's sons. Their story demonstrates to us that God moves in mysterious ways. He may seem unconventional, even radical, at times. But just as in the lives of Rachel and Leah, God is always in control.

He loves you and me so much and wants only what is best for us.

CHAPTER SIX:

Game Changer Moment

"She who was barren has borne seven children."
– 1 Samuel 2:5

In the first book of Samuel, the Bible recounts the story of Hannah, a God-fearing woman who is deeply anguished by her state of barrenness. As I read Hannah's story, I could identify with her pain and empathize with her trouble. But beyond Hannah's suffering, I could also see once again the power of the Almighty working subtly behind the scene, molding and shaping Hannah to get her to a place where God could use her for a very important assignment.

Through one very special declaration, Hannah's circumstances shifted. Something bigger than just conception unfolded in Hannah's life. God was again demonstrating that he moves in mysterious ways. This was Hannah's game-changer moment.

The story starts with an Israelite from the tribe of Ephraim named Elkanah who had two wives, Peninnah and Hannah. Peninnah, the second wife, had children, but Hannah had none, for she was barren. Still, as with Rachel and Leah, Elkanah loved Hannah best. Each year, the family would travel to Shiloh, where God's Tabernacle was pitched, to offer sacrifices to God. Now we come to the crux of the story:

> Whenever the day came for Elkanah to sacrifice, he would give portions of the meat to his wife Peninnah and to all her sons and daughters. But to Hannah he gave a double portion because he loved her, and the Lord had closed her womb.

126

Because the Lord had closed Hannah's womb, her rival kept provoking her in order to irritate her. This went on year after year. Whenever Hannah went up to the house of the Lord, her rival provoked her till she wept and would not eat. (1 Samuel 1:4-7)

The life Hannah shared with Peninnah was not at all pleasant. Peninnah must have felt very threatened and jealous of Hannah to harass a woman already weighed down by such a burden of barrenness. Her rival's taunting comments in addition to being barren must have been more than Hannah could bear. It is little wonder that Hannah's heart was so aggrieved.

I cannot imagine going through my nine-year infertility journey with provocative, mocking remarks from a friend or family member. The experience of infertility alone is painful enough. I can almost hear some of Peninnah's contemptuous remarks about her own ability to conceive whilst Hannah remained childless. It must have greatly tested Hannah's faith.

But just as we've already seen in the story of Rachel and Leah, God moves unexpectedly at times. Sometimes, as was the case for Jamie and me, God uses our pain and sufferings to grow and mature us. Although going through a trial is never fun, I discovered so much through my painful circumstances, and it was grief over my infertility that brought me to the end of myself. In Hannah's circumstances, I think the sorrow she encountered as a barren woman helped mold her for a very important mission.

Hannah's story continues with her earnest pleading year after year for God to answer her prayers for a baby. Her husband Elkanah was distressed by the pain his wife was suffering, as we can see in his comments:

Her husband Elkanah would say to her, "Hannah, why are you weeping? Why don't you

eat? Why are you downhearted? Don't I mean
more to you than ten sons?" (1 Samuel 1:8)

Such comments are familiar words for me. Jamie
would often try to console my aching heart with similar
terms of endearment. But no words of comfort could
assuage the longing I had for a child. As well-meaning as
Jamie was, his affirmation was no consolation for my
desperate need to be a mother. Hannah felt the same way.
She was aggrieved for the son she desperately wanted. She
was also tormented by years of Peninnah's harassment.

Hannah needed something to change. Year after
year her circumstances remained the same. Her prayers did
not seem to evoke any change of heart from God. Her rival
wasn't moved to compassion by her bleak situation. No
amount of offerings to God up at the Tabernacle seemed to
matter. Something different had to happen.

Then came one evening that changed Hannah's life
forever. The family had traveled to the Tabernacle for their

annual sacrifice. That evening after dinner, Hannah went up to the Tabernacle and in a deeply grief-stricken state made a declaration to God. That declaration was her game-changer moment:

> O Lord Almighty, if you will only look upon your servant's misery, and remember me, and not forget your servant but give her a son, then I will give him to the Lord for all the days of his life, and no razor will ever be used on his head.
> (1 Samuel 1: 9-11)

This dedication prayer changed everything. For years Hannah had asked God to answer her prayers for a child. But on this particular night, she made a new request. At this moment, while deep in heartfelt prayer and worship, something stirred in Hannah's heart. Something altered Hannah's thinking. She went from just asking to now offering.

I believe that God was bringing Hannah to this place of surrender where she could make such a special vow. It would take a strong and courageous woman to dedicate her son to be raised to live and worship God at the Tabernacle rather than be raised by his mother. I think that Hannah's dismal circumstances were preparing her for this unique assignment. Had she been capable of bearing children from the start, I wonder whether she could have offered this sacrifice to God. I wonder if this was part of God's plan for her family in the first place.

Possibly God had been waiting for this moment of declaration by Hannah and had been preparing her heart to get her to this yielding point. If Hannah had not experienced years of grief and heartache, perhaps she would not have offered such a vow.

Surrendering to Jesus was a pivotal point in my own journey. It was my own game-changer moment. For years I had grasped at earthly solutions, seeking medical assistance, charting my course, hoping such methods would be my answer. But they were not the solution God had in mind for Jamie and me. God had a different plan for our lives, one that required trusting in him completely for the healing of my womb. Once I laid down these earthly solutions and entered into a journey of faith with God, which I will share in succeeding chapters, God could begin to move accordingly in my life.

Hannah too needed to get to the end of herself before God's master plan, not just for her own life but her son's, could be revealed. I think we sometimes forget that the journey of parenthood is not only about us, but also involves our children to come. Hannah's dedication moment was essential and perfectly timed in order to bring about her firstborn child, who would lead a very anointed life. Likewise, my three children were born with purpose and in the Father's perfect timing.

While Hannah was offering her dedication prayer to God, the current high priest serving at the tabernacle, named Eli, was observing her. At first Eli assumed from Hannah's emotional outburst to God that she was drunk. But Hannah quickly made clear that she was sober and simply praying out of a deeply troubled and heartbroken place. Hannah's heartfelt prayer moved the priest as we see next in the passage:

> Eli answered, "Go in peace, and may the God of Israel grant you what you have asked of him." She said, "May your servant find favor in your eyes." Then she went her way and ate something, and her face was no longer downcast. (1 Samuel 1:17-18)

Hannah left the Tabernacle a very different person. Remember that year after year as Hannah went up to the Tabernacle, she couldn't eat due to her distress. Something has now changed because Hannah immediately goes and eats something. She is no longer saddened. Hannah had a new conviction. I believe it started with her declaration. This game-changer moment gave her clarity and a new confidence in her situation. For so many years, Hannah had simply cried out for deliverance, but God needed her to go deeper. To go on a journey that was exclusive to her.

Hannah's story reiterates how personal the barrenness journey really is. It is so unique and intimate. For me, and certainly for Hannah, it required a close relationship with God. There may not be one single game-changer moment for every couple trying to conceive. But for Jamie and me, it was not until we sat at the feet of Jesus that we were positioned to receive what he desired to offer us. Hannah's game-changer moment also occurred in the presence of the Lord.

Hannah had experienced so much heartache throughout her barrenness years. But thankfully, as Scripture tells us:

The Lord is close to the broken-hearted and saves those who are crushed in spirit. (Psalm 34:18).

By positioning herself again and again in front of God, pleading her case before him, Hannah eventually received what she had asked for and discovered her calling. Hannah became a mum! And in return for the blessing of motherhood, Hannah kept her vow to God and dedicated her firstborn son, Samuel, to the Lord all the days of his life. Samuel went on to lead a very special prophetic ministry, and he had a strong anointing of the Holy Spirit over his life. His mother's declaration was essential for the ministry Samuel would lead.

Hannah's testimony is proof that our current circumstances, however difficult and painful, may be essential to bringing about future good God has planned for our lives. I know that was the case for us. Infertility was the painful necessity that brought about Jamie's and my complete healing.

I hope Hannah's story will encourage you to continue to press closer to Jesus, seeking clarification from him for your situation. God may want to guide you into your very own game-changer moment. For me, there was a pivotal shift that took place in my life and heart when I surrendered all to Jesus, and I know this was my game-changer moment.

Hannah may have experienced a great deal of suffering in her pursuit to have a baby, but through her perseverance and by staying close to God, waiting, listening for his instruction and truth, she eventually discovered her calling. It was after this game-changer moment that Hannah received the healing she desperately sought and went on to be a mother of four sons and two daughters, including her firstborn, Samuel.

Hannah's story concludes the chapters dedicated to three of the six women in the Bible identified as being barren. Sarah, Rachel, and Hannah each had their own exceptional journey. They represent women going through barrenness right around the world today. It was through their testimonies that I found courage to pursue God for the healing of my own womb. And I hope they have been a source of encouragement for you as well.

Part II of *Having Faith* covers a season in my spiritual walk when my faith was being further refined by my Creator. It was a season of discovery that took me to higher grounds and ultimately led me into a deeper, more intimate relationship with the Trinity of God.

The first chapter of this section offers an overview of my faith journey through three different stages that were essential for my healing progression. In what I affectionately call my *ASK Trifecta*, I will explain each phase of my time spent *asking*, *seeking* and *knocking*, all of which were necessary to bring about the freedom I desperately sought. Following from there, I will then go into a little more detail about some of the lessons I was taught throughout my faith journey which segue into my happily-ever-after ending and my new life as a mum.

PART TWO:

Higher Ground

CHAPTER SEVEN:

My Ask Trifecta

"Ask and it will be given to you; Seek and you will find; Knock and the door will be opened to you, for everyone who asks receives; he who seeks finds; and to him who knocks, the door will be opened."

— Matthew 7:7-8

My youngest child, Levi, has a system in which to gain my attention. His first method is to yell out to me with a simple "Mum!" This intensifies the longer I don't respond. Eventually, if no answer is forthcoming, Levi will begrudgingly vacate what he is doing and come searching for me, still yelling out my name, but in a voice increasingly more impatient and annoyed.

If I happen to be in my bedroom with the door locked shut, Levi does not assume this means I am unavailable. Instead, he knocks repetitively, calling out my name even more intensely. This frenzy Levi has worked himself into suggests to me that something dreadful has happened. So I swiftly open the door to him, anxious and concerned. What I am confronted with instead is typically some simple question like "Can I have a sandwich?"

Levi's attention-seeking system reminds me of the three phases I went through in my healing journey, which at times proved equally tantrum-like. Like Levi, I found myself asking, seeking, and knocking until God opened the door for me.

The first of my three phases, *asking,* was simply a season of praying. I knew of no other method in which to beseech God to answer my prayer for a baby. So in this phase, possibly similar to Hannah's prayers before her game-changer moment, I found myself wearing out the floorboards in my house as I alternated between kneeling and pacing through innumerous amounts of prayers, begging incessantly for a miracle.

At some point around 2002, the asking phase seemed to have exhausted itself, and I realized I needed to go beyond that approach. I entered a second stage whereby I went looking for the source behind my healing needs. Akin to Levi seeking out his mother, I went searching for God's truth. I found God's Son, Jesus to be my answer. With Jesus as the key to answering my prayers, I eventually entered a third phase of knocking repeatedly at God's door. Just as my youngest son knocks at my door until I open it up, I was equally persistent with God.

My three-phase discovery journey, which I have named my *ASK Trifecta*, actually parallels the "ask, seek, knock" parable Jesus told in his Sermon on the Mount:

> Ask and it will be given to you; seek and you
> will find; knock and the door will be opened to

you. For everyone who asks receives; the one who seeks finds; and to the one who knocks, the door will be opened. (Matthew 7:7-8)

My ASK Trifecta followed the same order as Jesus describes in his parable, and each phase seemed to evolve into the next one at the perfect time. Not unlike my son Levi's attempt to gain my attention, there was a progression that took place in my healing season that began at asking and finished with God opening the door for me.

The first stage in my ASK Trifecta, as I described earlier, was a season of asking. This phase was the most elementary but no less important phase of the trifecta. It was a season during which I simply prayed and asked God to heal my womb.

Asking began almost immediately upon Jamie and me realizing that we were infertile in 1998. Although we had not yet reconciled our marriage nor returned to our heavenly Father after leaving our previous church denomination, nevertheless Jamie and I still believed in the healing touch of God, and so we both sought it from him.

Between 1998 and 2002, during which period our attention was focused mostly on medically-assisted fertility treatments, our asking phase remained at quite a rudimentary level. We had not yet experienced true intimacy with Jesus, so asking in prayer was all we understood. But by 2002 Jamie and I had recommitted ourselves to God, and we had also chosen to relinquish full control of our fertility situation to him. As our spiritual awareness grew in maturity, our asking soon deepened into a time of intense prayer.

Over the next three years, Jamie and I began to pray somewhat differently. Instead of only asking for healing, of which we still did a lot, we also began to seek out God's truth concerning fertility. I spent much time searching Scripture and confessing God's Word into my prayer life.

The asking stage, which developed naturally into a season of seeking, was a foundational component of the ASK Trifecta, since our asking did not cease until we realized we were pregnant in January, 2006. Just as my son calls out my name until he gets an answer from me, I too did not stop asking God for the healing of my womb at any point in my journey. Instead, I continued asking God to answer my prayers for a baby right through the seeking and knocking stages as well. I think that is why the acronym *ASK* is so fitting for my journey as asking is present throughout all three stages.

Asking is sometimes all that is required. We don't always need to go beyond that first phase. I have had many experiences of answered prayers that have not required seeking and knocking. But for the healing of my womb, the asking stage eventually ran its course. As I mentioned before, I needed to go deeper. To discover why healing wasn't forthcoming when Jamie and I were continuously asking the ultimate Healer to heal me.

The wart that appeared on my finger in 2002, which I wrote about in an earlier chapter, began a three-year season of searching for answers. I went beyond the simple approach of asking and moved into a time of seeking.

Seeking took my faith walk to higher ground. In fact, a number of dreams I had during this season were centered on heights way beyond my comfort zone but which ultimately led me to trust Jesus in everything I do. I will detail over the next few chapters some of what I learned during my seeking phase. But in this section I want to focus on two areas that probably eclipse everything else I learned. My seeking phase consisted of *truth* and *intimacy*.

The more time I spent reading God's Word (truth), the more intimate my relationship with the Trinity of God became. And the more cherished God became to me (intimacy), the greater I comprehended his truth.

The seeking stage began the process of coming to understand God's plan and purpose for Jamie's and my marriage, our spiritual walk, and our individual lives. As I forged a deep and personal relationship with the Trinity of God, I began to trust that God's plans were indeed perfect. And as my trust grew, so too did the frequency of the time I spent in God's presence. Truth and intimacy positioned me to receive any instruction Jesus wanted to impart to me. I love the passage in the gospel of John where Jesus describes himself as the shepherd and us as his sheep:

> I am the good shepherd. The good shepherd lays
> down his life for the sheep . . . My sheep listen
> to my voice; I know them, and they follow me.
> (John 10:11, 27)

By placing myself close to Jesus, I learned to know my Shepherd's voice. This was an integral part of my journey, as every directive I received related to my healing came from this close relationship with my Shepherd. One such dream that exemplifies my deep and growing love and affection for my Shepherd occurred in the month of February, 2004. This dream demonstrates the frantic yearning I felt to pursue and seek my Savior during a season in my life when I was completely desperate for his truth to be revealed.

To set the scene a little bit, the era in which my dream took place was the nineteenth century, the location a beautiful, grandiose old mansion. I had been invited by the heir of the estate to attend a wedding there, and I along with all the other guests wore the opulent formal wear of that period, top hats and waist coasts for the men, corsets and hooped skirts for the women.

My dream began with me being greeted by an elderly butler who wished to show me where the reception banquet was taking place. I thanked him, noted where the reception room was located, but kept right on walking purposefully, desperately seeking out the heir of the estate.

In my pursuit, I came to a large, ornate ballroom.

The ballroom was empty except for a grand staircase that rose up along one side of the hall. Each flight of steps appeared to be made of pure gold. So did the railing, which was also laced with precious jewels such as rubies, sapphires, and emeralds. Light and colours of the rainbow drew my eyes up the staircase, which extended onward beyond the building, stretching heavenward. To say it was breathtaking does not do this staircase justice. Otherworldly is the only way to describe it.

The ballroom was no longer empty. A childhood friend and her brother approached, wanting to show me another area of the mansion. But I was resolved not to let anyone distract me from my purpose. You see, I had fallen in love with the heir of the estate, and I desperately needed to find him again. I could not wait another minute to be in his presence. I would keep seeking him out until I found him, and nothing and no one would get in my way.

This dream captured the very essence of my deep and growing love for Jesus, my Lord and King. My need to keep seeking him, searching for truth, abiding in his presence alone epitomizes my seeking phase perfectly. *Truth* and *intimacy* were wed together, as represented in this dream. The seeking stage is also designed for finding something, as we read in Proverbs:

> It is the glory of God to conceal a matter; to search out a matter is the glory of kings. (Proverbs 25:2)

This proverb reminds me of my middle son Joel's sixth birthday party. Jamie and I had arranged a surprise treasure hunt out in a nearby forest. We spent a week planning the surprise, and we had as much fun in the organizing of it as Joel and his guests enjoyed attending it.

In the planning stage, Jamie and I drew up a detailed treasure map along with fun clues to help the kids find the hidden treasure. We created fun activities and treats that Jamie planted along the course to motivate the children to keep going. On the day of the birthday party, the children all set out with their treasure maps and pirate paraphernalia in pursuit of the long-lost treasure chest.

The group, which included a couple of extra dads along with Jamie, walked the muddy forest floor for two hours. They all climbed over logs, along rickety railway tracks, and through a long, dark tunnel, earnestly seeking their goal. When at last they reached the final clue and the treasure was in their grasp, elation erupted among the group. Finally, each child could rest as they had found what they sought.

For Jamie and me, it was our *glory to conceal* the treasure chest for the birthday party. For Joel and his friends, it was their *glory to search out* the treasure through the clues we provided. Similarly, in my seeking stage, every time I searched for God's truth, he revealed another clue that ultimately led to discovering that Jesus was my treasure. Just as Joel's friends all rested at the finish line, enjoying the fruit (or rather, sweets, as the treasure turned out to be) of their labor, I too could rest once I had found my treasure chest, Jesus. God wants us to seek him and to find him. He promises to those who do pursue him:

> Whoever finds me finds life and receives favor
> from the Lord. (Proverbs 8:35)

By searching for answers, I came to experience extraordinary intimacy with Jesus. He was and remains to this day my treasure chest. While much still remained for the healing of my womb, it was Jesus whom I needed to allow to initiate that process. My role in the seeking phase was first of all to find Jesus. He promises to anyone who seeks him out:

I love those who love me, and those who seek

me find me. (Proverbs 8:17)

My second role in this seeking phase involved relinquishing control and allowing Jesus the liberty to govern my life completely. As I've mentioned in previous chapters, surrendering was not easy for me, but it was part of the trusting process I needed to learn in order to get me to higher grounds.

My final and third role during this seeking season involved learning simply to be still and listen, ready to move on Jesus's command. Only once I'd learned to dwell in a place of submission did my role become more active. But this became possible only because I was now operating out of the right system, one that included God's perfect timing and his perfect directives.

Knocking was the final stage of my ASK Trifecta. It became evident to me that I was entering into this new and final phase around the time I received from the Holy Spirit a scripture verse along with associated dreams I will share with you in the next chapter:

> Therefore, since we are surrounded by such a great cloud of witnesses, let us throw off everything that hinders and the sin that so easily entangles. And let us run with perseverance the race marked out for us, fixing our eyes on Jesus, the pioneer and perfecter of faith. (Hebrews 12:1-2b)

Knocking is the persistent phase. As this scripture reminds us, running the race marked out for us requires determination and perseverance. Preparing well for my race, even starting it brilliantly, would have been of little use if I didn't finish the race according to God's plan for my life. Finishing the race well was integral for my journey. Otherwise I would not have received what God had planned for me.

–Having Faith–

Determination has always been one of my strengths. Like a bull terrier, once I get focused on a mission, I don't quit. I remember at age sixteen during my last year of high school when I decided to take on the Bronze Medallion challenge, which is the global yardstick for life-savers and a prerequisite for Australia's Surf Life Savers. I loved the idea of becoming a surf life saver, so I began the grueling three-month training program. But as soon as I started, I wanted to give up.

Every Sunday morning throughout the winter months, I had to be down at one of Queensland's Gold Coast beaches, about forty minutes from where I lived in Brisbane, ready to battle cold, rough seas. It was physically exhausting, and I found it absolute torture. But though others in the group chose to quit, I did not. I didn't enjoy the experience, but nevertheless I persevered till the end, earning the prized bronze medallion that awarded me the title of Surf Life Saver.

This same determination helped me to persevere and remain steadfast during the last leg of my barrenness journey. Ironically, the knocking phase really does require knocking. It reminds me of a time in my childhood when I would go around my neighborhood knocking at doors, trying to sell chocolates to raise funds for my school. Sometimes I would knock at a neighbor's front door, but there would be no response. All signs of life suggested someone was home, so instead of accepting that perhaps they didn't want to be disturbed and I should move on to the next house, I would persistently keep on knocking until someone eventually succumbed and opened the door.

I believe this is what we are called to do with God. We are to keep knocking, pursuing him even when it seems he isn't going to answer the door. Just as the person inside the house might have heard me knocking but either wouldn't or couldn't come to the door, so God may have his reason for not opening the door as swiftly as we would like. In my circumstances, God was doing a mad-dash cleanup—not of my home, but of me!—so would open the door only when he considered the timing to be right.

This knocking season kept me taking my concerns constantly to God. Once my youngest son Levi would find me (the seeking phase), he would then knock doggedly until I eventually opened the door for him. Once I'd gone through my own season of seeking, in which I'd discovered Jesus to be the key to my healing needs, my knocking simply kept my desire at the forefront before God. By the end of this seeking phase, I had grown confident in the journey I had experienced with God, so as I entered this new season, I simply followed what Scripture says:

> So do not throw away your confidence; it will be richly rewarded. You need to persevere so that when you have done the will of God, you will receive what he has promised. (Hebrews 10:35)

While in this season of knocking, I found myself pursuing God even more. My pursuit of God at this point was not just to seek, but rather to engage and follow God, constantly bathing in his presence, regardless of any apparent result. And God wants us to do that. After all God knocks on our hearts too. He knows all too well about constant knocking and trying to gain our attention, as we read in the Bible's very last book, Revelation:

> Here I am! I stand at the door and knock. If anyone hears my voice and opens the door, I will come in and eat with that person, and they with me. (Revelations 3:20)

When I pursued God, knocking repetitively at his door, God heard my daily cries and swiftly answered my request. Granted, a nine-year journey may not seem all that swift. But throughout those many years, God was healing me continuously, leading to the ultimate healing of my womb.

–Having Faith–

Continuous knocking shows tenacity and resolve. It is a demonstration of faith in action. When I went door-knocking as a youngster, when my son Levi knocks doggedly on my bedroom door, it is because we both have a purpose. I knocked on God's door for the same reason. I had a purpose, and I wanted to be invited into his plan for my life. The good news is that God wants us to knock on his door and he can't wait to open it for us.

I admit that at times it felt as though my knocks were going unanswered, even ignored. But that's only because we don't see what is actually happening behind the door, which is God preparing the way. By continually knocking and waiting with expectation for the door to be opened, I was in time overwhelmingly blessed, as Proverbs 8:34 promises:

> Blessed is the man [or woman] who listens to Me, watching daily at My doors, waiting at My doorway [emphasis mine].

Throughout our barrenness journey, Jamie and I were given two symbolic pictures that represented the spiritual cause of our infertility. The first, a lock over my womb, was more like a visual impression Jamie and I both sensed that was preventing our conceiving. I mentioned this lock imagery briefly in an earlier chapter as having helped birth my faith journey.

This symbolic lock was later identified a second time in a vision by the pastor of a church that was holding a prayer-healing night which we attended. The pastor prayed over me, releasing this lock, during my seeking phase in April, 2005. I knew the lock was now opened because this initiated a new phase of revelations for me. It was also confirmed in a dream I received later that year, which I will tell you about later.

But Jamie and I also received a second pictorial image shortly after that symbolic lock was opened over my womb. This time the symbol came through our mentor friend Bob while we were all praying together. During our prayer time, Bob saw a vision of a closed door over my womb that was also locked. This door remained shut over my womb for many months during the seeking phase and throughout my time of knocking. Among other things, the door was indicative of my knocking phase, and it reminded me that behind the closed door God was working tirelessly on my behalf.

Meanwhile as I was knocking constantly on God's door, God was preparing a way to open it for me as swiftly as possible. And as is God's perfect way, once I did receive my final deliverance, as I will tell you about later, we received a final symbolic image given in a pictorial vision to the very pastor who had previously prayed for the release of the lock over my womb. That image was that of an open door!

My ASK Trifecta represents the overall picture of my barrenness journey. Each season taught me invaluable lessons and ultimately paved the way for Jesus's healing. When I asked, God answered. When I sought truth, I found Jesus to be my answer. And when I knocked, God swung the door open for me at the perfect time. And I am not the exception. God promises the same for each and every one of his children as we've already seen Jesus declare in the conclusion to his "ask, seek, knock" parable:

> For everyone who asks receives; the one who seeks finds; and to the one who knocks, the door will be opened. (Matthew 7:8)

Over the next few chapters, I will share some of the lessons I learned during my seeking phase and which make up my season of discovery. Every lesson and principle that God shared with me was relevant to my healing needs and marked the faith journey I was embarked on. I hope that my discovery season will resonate on some level with your own and that it will encourage you to pursue Jesus in your own walk.

CHAPTER EIGHT:

Make Me a Woman of Faith

"Now faith is being sure of what we hope for and certain of what we do not see. This is what the ancients were commended for."

— Hebrews 11:1

When I was about fourteen years of age, I made a strange request. I asked God to make me a woman of faith. I was in church listening to a message on faithfulness when my heart began to stir. The preacher was speaking on the biblical story of Ruth, a Moabite widow who showed extraordinary devotion and faithfulness to her mother-in-law, Naomi. If you haven't already read Ruth's story, I would definitely encourage you to do so. Ruth's story of courage and faithfulness activated something deep inside me, inspiring me to want a faith journey of my own.

I know I was young and naïve when I made that prayer. Still, even as a teenager I fully understood what I was asking God for. A faith like Ruth's, which was exhibited by following God regardless of what that looked like, moved my heart, triggering deep within me this desire to be such a woman of faith.

As time went by, I forgot about this teenage request. It wasn't until March, 2002, about twelve years later, that God reminded me of it through a very simple dream in which God lovingly told me, "You are like Ruth." This gentle reminder of my adolescent aspirations to be like my Bible favourite Ruth once again deeply moved my spirit. The dream also coincided with the appearance on my finger of the little wart I wrote about earlier.

The combination of this wart, which was symbolic of the faith encounter I'd had as a six-year-old child, and a dream that bespoke my teenage desire to be a woman of faith strengthened and encouraged me to enter a new faith journey with God. It is that faith appointment I want to share more of in this section of the book.

Over the next few chapters, I will share some of what I learned during this season that transformed forever my spiritual life. If you too are undergoing a time in the wilderness, I pray that my faith story will encourage you to trust and seek Jesus for clarity in your own walk.

Just as barrenness is individual and personal to every couple experiencing it, so too is any form of healing. I have said it a number of times before, but it is important for me to emphasize this message again: God deals with us all differently. Every couple experiencing infertility has their own unique story, and each situation requires its own touch by God. There is no one-size-fits-all scenario, and my own story is no different. It is exclusive to Jamie and me.

I do not subscribe to any prescribed formula that guarantees healing. The principles I share are not offered as a set of instructions that will guarantee anyone else's healing from infertility. They form part of my testimony and are therefore significant to this book. Ultimately, Jesus is our Healer, and he alone holds the key. The barrenness journey is hard enough as it is without feeling self-condemnation if healing is not forthcoming. Healing comes in many forms and is in the hands of our Savior Jesus Christ. No set of instructions will ever change that.

Faith, I now realize, has woven itself consistently throughout my life. But in relation to my nine-year journey of infertility, it really became active from 2002 onward. Faith empowered me to combat doubt and disbelief, two strong emotions that were my constant enemy as we will discuss in the next chapter. And along with perseverance, faith became my integral companion, especially during my last couple years of barrenness.

Between the years 2001 through 2006, God gained my attention through various means. Sometimes I received dreams and visions. At other times I would receive a timely, encouraging word, scripture, or prophetic visualisation such as the unlocking of my womb. All of which inspired Jamie and me to stay the course.

But during this season there were also many valley moments when everything went still and quiet and God seemed unattainable. During those moments, I needed to rely on faith. Scripture describes for us just what this is:

> Now faith is being sure of what we hope for and
> certain of what we do not see. (Hebrews 11:1)

This statement actually sums up our Christian call perfectly—to believe in the Lord Jesus Christ as our Savior even though we may not personally see him. But this scripture also impels me to consider exactly what I was so sure and certain of during my season in the wilderness. And that was a very strong conviction that God had created me to be a mother. Even as a young girl, I had been confident this was God's calling for me. I was also certain that the key to unlocking my fertility was in God's hand. After relinquishing earthly methods in 2002, I no longer had medical options available to me, so my certainty had to come from the healing touch of God alone.

But not every couple wanting children may be given the same assurance. I asked a friend going through her own infertility struggles what she could be sure of. She stated simply her assurance of how much God loved her. That was enough for her. Because of God's love for her, she could rest assured that her situation was in his divine plan for her life. That her assurance is different than mine doesn't mean she has less or more faith. It is simply that— different!

Another friend believed wholeheartedly that God could and would use medical intervention to aid her efforts to conceive. She is now mother to a beautiful son, and she gives God all the glory. In all these scenarios, each woman, including myself, had different assurances. But we were each still sure of what we hoped for. Having such an assurance enabled faith to reign in my life even when my physical reality was presenting me with the opposite.

Part of my own assurance came from my fundamental belief in who God had created me to be, which was a mother. But I would be foolish to hang all my hopes on a whim. For my faith walk, I needed to delve deeper into the Bible, unearthing truth from God's Word. Truth which I hoped would confirm my conviction that I was born to procreate.

And sure enough, I discovered so many beautiful passages that reiterated God's plan for mankind to "bear fruit and multiply" (Genesis 1:22, 28; 9:7; Leviticus 26:9; Deuteronomy 7:13; etc.). By reading and embedding God's truths into my everyday living, I was able to oppose any disbelief that emerged to shake my confidence in what God had called me to be.

The inspired Word of God offered great comfort and hope to Jamie and me, especially when our faith was feeling weakened. This often happened in the aftermath of friends and family procreating with seemingly little or no effort. Being invited to dinner parties where we were surrounded by couples talking about their pregnancies or young children generated overwhelming thoughts of rejection and despondence. I often came away deeply crushed and discouraged, the contrast of our own situation eroding my faith. By keeping God's Word close, I could combat those negative emotions. The Bible is truth, and reading God's truth brought me hope so I could believe in what I couldn't see.

But although having an assurance in what we hope for is good, and embedding Scripture into our hearts and minds to reinforce this belief is hugely beneficial, the more

I continued along my faith journey, the more I realised how little this journey was about me. Instead, my testimony was a story of the faithfulness of my Lord Jesus Christ, as is illustrated in the following passage:

> Therefore, since we are surrounded by such a great cloud of witnesses, let us throw off everything that hinders and the sin that so easily entangles. And let us **run with perseverance** the race marked out for us. Let us **fix our eyes on Jesus**, the author and perfecter of our faith, who for the joy set before him endured the cross, scorning its shame, and sat down at the right hand of the throne of God. Consider him who endured such opposition from sinful men, so that you will not grow weary and lose heart. (Hebrews 12:1-3)

God used this passage to shift my focus away from me and what I needed to *do,* showing me that it is Jesus who created and makes perfect our faith. It has nothing to do with us, but everything to do with him. In this passage of Scripture, the only part we play is to fix our eyes on Jesus. By focusing completely on who Jesus is and what he came to do on our behalf, I could run my own race with perseverance.

The establishment of a deep and very personal relationship with the Son of God was essential in growing my faith. For those who have grown up with Jesus as their Lord and Savior, you are already many steps ahead of where I was. As you know by now, Jamie and I had a warped belief system built entirely around Old Testament teachings that were legalistic by nature with a sin/repent focus. So forming an intimate, loving relationship with Jesus, one that was not centred on our need to earn his approval was an integral step in our faith walk for both Jamie and me.

Throughout 2001-2003, I received a number of dreams that reiterated Jesus's desire to become my friend. I remember one such dream in 2003 where I was handed some earrings made out of crystal that had been sitting on a little stand in the shape of a cross. In the dream, I initially didn't want to accept the earrings and felt judged by the person presenting them to me. I felt a lot of shame due to the years I'd distanced myself from my heavenly Father, and in this dream my guilt overwhelmed me. But once I realized the person presenting me these beautiful earrings had no agenda nor desire to judge me, I became overcome with gratitude and willing to accept the gift.

This dream typified the wonderful gift Jesus has given to us, not only by dying on the cross for us (symbolized in my dream as a cross-shaped stand), but by presenting himself as a precious gift (the crystal earrings) and friend to us all. In this dream, Jesus supplanted my shame with his own grace. He later revealed to me that the crystal from which the earrings were made represented his purity and healing touch. This inspired our daughter Faith's middle name, Crystal.

Through the many dreams I received, which drew me closer to Jesus, through reading the gospels and listening to sound New Testament teachings, as well as through much prayer and worship, I came to accept Jesus's unconditional love for me. From that foundational perspective, I could then trust in Jesus to be my conqueror, my restorer, my healer, and my dearest friend. By spending time in this new and wonderful relationship with Jesus, both Jamie and I were able to remain steadfast in our pursuit for the healing of my womb.

My relationship with the Holy Spirit also became very intimate, especially during the last leg of my journey. God desires a close relationship with each of his children. He demonstrated this in the Garden of Eden when he walked and talked with Adam and Eve in the cool of the day (Genesis 3:8). The Holy Spirit is ever approachable and available, and he is patiently desiring to commune with each one of us on a personal level.

It was the support and encouragement Jamie and I received from the Holy Spirit that enabled us to persevere for so long. The Holy Spirit was my encourager, supporter, and the wisdom behind my journey. The Holy Spirit became a truly intimate, loving confidant whom I love deeply to this day. He was also represented in many of my dreams, particularly throughout 2005, as either a stirring wind or flooding water.

In one such dream, I was walking along the streets of Melbourne with a female friend when a piece of paper floated down from heaven. It read simply, "Jesus loves you." These words were always a poignant reminder for me, and the Holy Spirit knew they would greatly encourage me at a point in my walk when the pain and reality of my situation was overwhelming me.

The dream then continued with a stirring of wind that blew paperwork and documents all around my girlfriend and me, each piece of paper holding a clue as to why I was infertile. My girlfriend and I couldn't decipher any of their script by ourselves, which in my dream was quite distressing to me. Just then we were approached by two men, my mentor friend Bob and a friend of his. Both men could decipher the sheets of paper they held and expressed astonishment at my inability to read them.

This dream was actually a follow-up from a dream I'd experienced a fortnight earlier in which I was given Bob's name to help me work through my infertility issues. Since I hadn't given the first dream enough consideration, a second dream proved necessary to gain my attention. Through this revelation in my second dream that Bob was capable of deciphering and interpreting, I recognized that the Holy Spirit was guiding me to work closely with Bob in translating the many dreams and visions I had received, all vital for my healing but which I was struggling to fully understand.

What I came to appreciate through this experience was that the Holy Spirit really does desire a relationship with each one of us. I was fortunate to receive a number of dreams that pointed to this. However, my relationship with the Holy Spirit only grew in strength as I spent quality time in praise, worship, and just basking in his presence. It was through the establishment of a personal relationship with the third Member of the Godhead that both Jamie and I were able to believe in the impossible.

In contrast to this divine support, people cannot always be that reliable. Sometimes as humans, well-meaning though we may be, we allow our own prejudices to get in the way of truth. And when truth is squashed, faith can become weakened. The Holy Spirit, in contrast, is perfect wisdom, perfect truth, and perfect love.

Perseverance was another essential element of my faith walk. It became particularly central during the final months when I felt my healing journey was coming to an end and I was in a place of waiting, i.e., my knocking phase. I've already mentioned the biblical command I received from Hebrews 12:1 to run my race with perseverance. This concept of running with perseverance became even more relevant in August, 2005, when I had a dream that I was running a race around a mountain, determined and resolved to finish.

Many of my friends and family were in the dream. They had all completed the event and were relaxing with their children at the finish line. I on the other hand was still running, persevering, exhausted, but determined to finish the race. And eventually I did. This dream encouraged me to persist, to not give up, to have faith that the battle was nearly won. And so it proved to be. Only months later, my wilderness days would be over.

I think it is important to emphasize the role perseverance played in my journey. It is one thing to have faith, but sometimes we need to combine that faith with steadfast pursuit until what we are asking for comes to pass. Seven months later during my first trimester of pregnancy, this truth was reiterated to me in a second dream of running a race around a mountain. This dream was much like the first one. But this time when I finished the race, I was met by a man who spoke these encouraging words to me: "You never gave up, you kept on running with perseverance, and you finished what no one thought you would."

Note that both faith and perseverance are *doing*, or action, words. With faith, we need to believe in something. With perseverance, we must carry that baton of faith until it comes to pass as the writer of Hebrews reminds us:

> Once you believe, you need to persevere so that when you have done the will of God, you will receive what he has promised. (Hebrews 10:36).

This scripture reiterated to me the effectiveness of applying both faith and perseverance in accordance with God's plan for our lives. At times, the only action required for faith to be effective is stillness. We are to position ourselves at the cross and simply wait. Jesus is always the pinnacle of our faith. Faith is not about us; it's all about Jesus. As I've also mentioned earlier, my faith increased when I sought out God's purpose for my life, and more often than not this happened in the still, quiet moments. Only Jesus can accomplish what we ask, and the moment I took my eyes off Christ, my faith would weaken and become fruitless.

But while faith is an action word, we don't necessarily need to muster up huge amounts of faith to receive healing from our Savior. In the New Testament book of Acts, we read of a crippled man who made his living as a beggar outside the temple. After he was healed by the apostle Peter in the name of Jesus, Peter explained to bystanders what had just happened:

> By faith in the name of Jesus, this man whom you see and know was made strong. It is Jesus's name and the faith that comes through him that has given this complete healing to him, as you can all see. (Acts 3:16)

Notice the phrase "and the faith that comes through him." This scripture doesn't state that healing came to the crippled man because of his own faith. Rather, the faith that healed him came through Jesus. In fact, the crippled man wasn't even seeking healing when he accosted Peter, but begging for money. It was Peter's conviction in the name of Jesus coupled with Jesus's faithfulness that brought about the miraculous healing of a man who had been crippled since birth. This story demonstrates that God's faithfulness abounds even when we do not seek it.

–Having Faith–

Active faith and perseverance were fundamental to my barrenness journey even in those times where all that was required of my faith was to remain still. One verse from the Psalms continually surfaced throughout my seeking and knocking phases, reminding me that when all seems silent God is often moving quite loudly in the background.

> Be still, and know that I am God; I will be exalted among the nations, I will be exalted in the earth. (Psalm 46:10)

My years of barrenness drew me into a faith journey with my Creator and helped me establish an intimate relationship with the Trinity of God. I became completely dependent on God to heal my womb, and out of that reliance I learned to trust God, to be still, and to wait with perseverance for God's divine intervention in my life. Without question, my faith in him became his faithfulness towards me!

Although as a fourteen-year-old I may not have understand just what was involved when I asked God to make me a woman of faith, I knew even then that's exactly who I was created to be. I was born to live a life marked by faith, and I was born to receive that faithfulness from the Author and Perfecter of our faith, Jesus Christ.

In the next chapter, I will share with you another principle I discovered during my seeking phase that helped develop and strengthen my faith, inspired by the writings of the apostle Paul in Ephesians 6. In this passage, Paul speaks of the armour of God, which helps us combat any attacks the devil sends our way. Through applying this spiritual metaphor, I began to combat some of the emotions and disabling lies that held me captive and to begin living in the freedom that Christ bought for us.

CHAPTER NINE:

Blueprint

"Put on the full armor of God so that you can take your stand against the devil's schemes." — Ephesians 6:10

For most of my barren years, I had an overwhelming energy of faith in the lead-up to ovulation day. But the moment I ovulated and entered the two-week "wait", the second half of the ovulation cycle, doubt and disbelief engulfed me. For some reason, I would lose all hope during this time, and a barrage of disheartening comments would whisper in my mind, saying, "Who are you kidding? Why would you expect this month to be any different than before? You're barren, so just except your fate and let it go!"

Discouragement was a very effective weapon against me, so Satan would feed me lies, drudging up past inadequacies that caused me to doubt my security in Christ. He would whisper to me that I was unworthy of becoming a mum. He would remind me of how many years had already gone by without my conceiving. If I was ever to win the battle against these mind games, I needed to learn how to combat this bombardment of negative and deceitful untruths that Satan cast my way month after month.

It was early 2004 when a volunteer came into my office at church and handed me a pamphlet. On the cover was a somewhat juvenile depiction of a soldier in full armour holding up shield and sword as though ready for battle. The pamphlet described in simple terminology the various pieces of spiritual armour the apostle Paul instructs Christians to put on in Ephesians 6:10-20, often referenced as the Armour of God passage.

I had read this passage before and even heard occasional messages on the topic. But it wasn't until I saw this simple illustration that I realized God has given us the blueprint of how to protect ourselves from the devil's schemes. Including the negative lies Satan was continuously firing at me. This spiritual armour metaphor became my answer as to how I could combat Satan and safeguard my heart while under attack.

In the passage, the apostle Paul describes six pieces of armour as being essential for us to wear in battle. Of course, he isn't speaking of a physical battle or armour made of some physical material. Rather, it is a spiritual battle:

> Our struggle is not against flesh and blood, but against the rulers, against the authorities, against the powers of this dark world and against the spiritual forces of evil in the heavenly realms. (Ephesians 6:12)

This spiritual struggle the apostle Paul described seemed to align with what Jamie and I had been feeling clear back to 2002, i.e., that our infertility was a spiritual lock that somehow needed to be opened. While our battle of infertility manifested itself physically, we had sensed for some time that my struggle to conceive was not a physical issue but spiritual by nature.

Part of this spiritual battle over my fertility was being governed by two strong emotions I've already described—doubt and disbelief. In permitting the devil's lies to bind me, I was preventing faith and hope from prevailing against their opposing negative emotions, especially in the second half of my monthly cycles. As Proverbs 13:12 tells us:

> Hope deferred makes the heart sick, but a
> longing fulfilled is a tree of life.

How true I found this to be! Doubt invokes hesitation, scepticism, and distrust. When these feelings struck at my heart, hope could not take root. Nor could faith do what it was created to do—believe that something we hope for will come to pass (Hebrew 11:1). But through the unwitting aid of a church volunteer, I was given the armour of God allegory to help me combat Satan's negative and debilitating lies that were conjuring up doubt and disbelief in my heart. The apostle Paul describes six pieces that make up the armour which are essential for our defence in combat:

> Therefore put on the **full armor of God**, so that when the day of evil comes, you may be able to stand your ground, and after you have done everything, to stand. Stand firm then, with the **belt of truth** buckled around your waist, with the **breastplate of righteousness** in place, and with your **feet fitted with** the readiness that comes from the **gospel of peace**. In addition to all this, take up the **shield of faith,** with which you can extinguish all the flaming arrows of the evil one.

Take the **helmet of salvation** and the **sword of the Spirit**, which is the word of God. (Ephesians 6:13-17)

What helped me put this spiritual metaphor into practice in my daily life was visualizing myself wearing each piece of armour mentioned in this passage. For me, the belt of truth illustrates the importance of separating the devil's lies from God's own counsel. It was very important for me to know whom I was listening to, especially when positioning myself to believe for something that was seemingly impossible. I've already mentioned that when I relied on human council, I often received mixed reviews. Some people supported our decision not to seek further infertility treatments while others encouraged us to pursue further medical intervention or adoption.

Jamie and I also received advice from well-meaning Christians suggesting that maybe it was God's will we remain barren. That perhaps God had a different plan for our future. When I relied on human support instead of the Holy Spirit's guidance, I often came away confused and disheartened by the conflicting messages my husband and I received. By visualising myself wearing the belt of truth, I could remain steadfast in the mission we had been given.

The helmet of salvation and breastplate of righteousness are parts of God's armour that substantiate my position in Christ. Visualizing myself wearing these pieces of armour reminds me that I am a saved, virtuous child of God and that my redemption has been completely bought and paid for by my Lord Jesus Christ. This was an especially important reminder for me given my legalistic upbringing and wayward behaviour prior to returning to my heavenly Father.

The example of feet fitted with the readiness that comes from the gospel of peace was another piece of armour essential to squash any fear and doubt that tried to surface. Through this visual aid, I drew on the peace that comes from the gospel message. A message of peace that is ours only through Jesus Christ.

The sword of the Spirit, which is the Word of God, also became increasingly important to me. Through the Holy Spirit's truth, I could live out a triumphant faith, which in turn helped defuse any doubt and disbelief that continued to wreak havoc in my mind. It was essential for me to replace the negative emotions of doubt and disbelief with the truth that comes from reading God's Word, the Bible. The sword of the Spirit realigned my thinking.

The final piece of armour referenced is the shield of faith, a spiritual metaphor that illustrates protecting oneself from the flaming arrows Satan throws our way. This particular imagery was crucial for me in combating the devil's lies, especially after so many months and years of being unable to conceive when Satan took pleasure in feeding me distrust and disparagement. With the shield of faith firmly in place, I could begin to ward off his lies and mocking remarks. I knew Satan hated the stance Jamie and I had taken in believing for the miraculous healing of my womb, therefore I also knew I needed to be vigilant in guarding my heart from his accusations.

Along with putting on these six pieces of protective armour, the apostle Paul also instructs us to add one more element in order to defend ourselves effectively against the enemy:

> And pray in the Spirit on all occasions with all
> kinds of prayers and requests. With this in mind,
> be alert and always keep on praying for all the
> Lord's people. (Ephesians 6:18)

As I learned to put on the armour of God, prayer became central to my spiritual walk. I didn't see prayer as some formalized spiritual ritual, although formal prayers have their place. Quite often my most effective prayer sessions, the ones where I most felt I'd heard from God, took place in the car on my way to work. By this time

Jamie and I had moved to a small town about forty minutes from my job, where we were building our new home. It was during this commute to and from work that I would enjoy my time of worship with God. Sometimes I would so get lost in prayer and worship that by the time I got to work I had no idea how I'd even arrived at my destination.

Prayer was the lifeblood of my mission and essential in growing my relationship with the Trinity of God. Prayer also became an intimate experience that Jamie and I enjoyed (and still do) together and which has helped shield us from the attacks of Satan.

Paul's Armour of God metaphor contains one final important element:

> Therefore put on the full armour of God, so that when the day of evil comes, you may be able to stand your ground, and after you have done everything, to stand. (Ephesians 6:13)

One thing I have learned through applying Paul's teaching in Ephesians 6 to my own life is the importance of being on guard at all times, ready to stand our ground in battle since we never know just when the enemy may attack. Especially when a child of God is believing for something that is contrary to what the devil would want. If I neglected to be on guard, Satan would once again try his favourite and most effective weapons against me—doubt and disbelief.

As I touched on earlier, that doubt sometimes came unintentionally from those closest to us. Frequently, I needed to measure whether a word from a friend, a voice in my head, other conversations I was having, or simply feelings and impressions I received were a word from God or a distraction from Satan. I could not achieve this without discernment from the Holy Spirit. Jamie and I often had to evaluate what we were hearing; distinguishing Satan's lies that contradicted the hope we had received from God. This was using the belt of truth in combat.

Sometimes I did let my guard down and forget to use the armour of God to defuse the enemy's lies. On one occasion in 2004, I had come to the end of my tether. I was tired of waiting on the Lord and ready to give up. I was also starting to distrust the faith conviction Jamie and I held. Yes, I had let doubt and disbelief run rampant in my head again.

But God, ever loving and faithful, drew me back once more. In another dream that didn't seem so important at the time, God took me back to 2002 when the wart had first appeared on my finger. God then reminded me that the wart was a symbol of the faith walk I was on and that I was to stand firm in faith and keep on persevering.

Another such moment when the weight and burden of barrenness seemed too much to bear came during our final year of infertility in early 2005. I had just gone through another monthly cycle without getting pregnant and for a time I became really angry at God for allowing me to go through such a painful experience. To make matters worse, Jamie and I were being bombarded with suggestions from friends and family to change the course of action we'd chosen to take. Often these suggestions involved adopting or looking after children in foster care, both loving options that played heavily on my conscience.

After eight long, lonely years, I don't know why the burden of infertility got the better of me this particular month. It didn't seem to matter that God had been so gracious with me, continually blessing me with words and dreams that encouraged me to stay the course. I started to wonder whether I was on the right path or whether after all the counsel we'd received from friends and family was God's answer.

I was also worried that my own pride might be preventing Jamie and me from receiving the blessing of parenthood through the means those closest to us were suggesting. Was I simply being stubborn in refusing a change of course? Still, stubborn or not, I could not shake the promises I was convinced God had given me from Scripture:

> If you, then, though you are evil, know how to give good gifts to your children, how much more will your Father in heaven give good gifts to those who ask him! (Matthew 7:11)

> Take delight in the Lord, and he will give you the desires of your heart. (Psalm 37:4).

I knew what the desires of my heart were—to conceive and bear naturally three children to my husband. And I'd felt confident that my heavenly Father wanted to give me this gift. Confused and weary, I asked God to show me which way Jamie and I were to go. Jamie continued to feel led to wait. I on the other hand was at another crossroad. I needed God's guidance to show me whether my own stubbornness was preventing us from receiving the gift we were waiting for.

God led me to the biblical story of Noah. As I read the passage, my eyes were opened to how Noah had built the ark in the midst of criticism, rejection, mocking remarks, and sniggering gestures. With all odds against him, despite ridicule and condemnation from his peers, Noah had remained faithful to God's promise of a coming flood.

Through this passage, God revived in me a willingness to wait on him, be patient, and endure the race set before us. I was able to raise again the shield of faith to defuse the fiery arrows being cast at me from every angle. And through the sword of the Spirit, the Word of God, I was encouraged to once again stand up and fight.

The spiritual metaphor the apostle Paul gives in Ephesians 6 of the armour of God was a wonderful visual aid that enabled me to combat Satan's attacks. Doubt and disbelief were my archenemies throughout my years of infertility. But by being aware of the spiritual battle going on around us and by covering myself with the full armour of God, I could extinguish doubt and disbelief, allowing faith instead to triumph.

God's blueprint of a spiritual armour helped me to take my stand against the devil's schemes (Ephesians 1:11). I hope our study of it in these pages will remind you that you are not alone either. God has provided to any of his children who will simply choose to cover themselves with it, his protective armour. God's armour is there to combat against evil. And along with that armour, we have our Savior and Shepherd Jesus Christ, who positions himself before and behind us, protecting and guarding us all the way.

But I was not yet finished with my healing journey, as I will share with you in the following chapter. Another essential part of my spiritual healing involved my speech, which in turn reflected the condition of my heart. My heart

was in poor condition, which resulted in an outpouring of

negative and destructive words that prevented me from

living in the fullness of God's blessings. In his mercy, God

revealed to me the errors of my ways and showed me how a

sick heart can be restored so that I might live from then on

in his abundance.

CHAPTER TEN:

Safeguard

"The tongue of the wise brings healing." — Proverbs 12:18

When Jamie and I were dating, we had our fair share of arguments. I couldn't tell you what any one of them was about. But I can remember blurting out a single sentence during one of our disagreements that became our relationship motto: "If what's on the tip of your tongue is not worth saying, swallow it!"

I must admit I haven't been great at adhering to my own wise counsel. It has always been much easier for me to verbalize whatever I am thinking or feeling. Although I spoke this proverb in anger to my future husband, even then Jamie and I both knew it applied more to my unguarded tongue than his. Enough so that a full eight years after spouting this one-liner, God had to remind me of my need to safeguard what kind of words emerged from my mouth.

It was through the teachings of James, brother of Jesus and author of the New Testament epistle bearing his name, that the Holy Spirit began transforming this aspect of my inner self and spiritual walk. This was now 2002, the fifth year of my infertility struggle, and over the years I had formed a very bad habit of speaking negatively about my reproductive system.

In fact, it began much earlier all the way back to when I started menstruating as a young teen. Each menstrual cycle I would experience enormous pain, which resulted in my cursing my womanhood. In those younger years, I would speak out angrily about having to be a female and endure both the inconvenience and extreme pain I suffered every month. I hated getting my period, and I begrudged the disruption to my teenage lifestyle of swimming and being carefree.

So when Jamie and I realized in 1998 that we were having problems conceiving, my natural response was to revert back to cursing my womanhood. I labeled myself as a woman incapable of bearing children. I also proclaimed aloud the medical verdict of *unknown infertility* into which the doctors had categorized Jamie and me. Out of ignorance, but no less mistakenly, I began to speak lies over my fruitfulness.

Typical phrases I spoke included: "I'm infertile. I can't have children. I'm never going to be a mum. I have unknown infertility. It's never going to happen for me." And the list could go on.

While I may have spoken such phrases with no ill intent, and in reality they were more likely intended to elicit sympathy than anything else, nevertheless they had an adverse effect over my life. A childhood lyric bantered around my schoolyard asserts, "Sticks and stones may hurt my bones, but words will never harm me." In reality, words do hurt and, as I discovered, must always be safeguarded. More so, our tongue needs safeguarding and kept in check. Here is what James had to say about the tongue:

> We all stumble in many ways. Anyone who is never at fault in what they say is perfect, able to keep their whole body in check. When we put bits into the mouths of horses to make them obey us, we can turn the whole animal. Or take ships as an example. Although they are so large and are driven by strong winds, they are steered by a very small rudder wherever the pilot wants to go. Likewise, the tongue is a small part of the body, but it makes great boasts. Consider what a great forest is set on fire by a small spark. The tongue also is a fire, a world of evil among the parts of the body. It corrupts the whole body, sets the whole course of one's life on fire, and is itself set on fire by hell. All kinds of animals, birds, reptiles and sea creatures are being tamed and

have been tamed by mankind, but no human being can tame the tongue. It is a restless evil, full of deadly poison.

Note that James describes the tongue as only a small part of our body, but with the capacity to govern our whole life, either for good or for evil. It can also corrupt our entire person and spew out deadly poison that will destroy everything and everyone in our path. James goes on to point out the hypocrisy with which we often use our tongue:

> With the tongue we praise our Lord and Father, and with it we curse human beings, who have been made in God's likeness. Out of the same mouth come praise and cursing. My brothers and sisters, this should not be. (James 3: 9-10)

When I first read the above passages in 2002, they really struck a chord with me. James's writings convicted me that my already unbridled tongue had become completely undisciplined. I realized that while I was praising God, I was in the very same breath cursing my own body made in his likeness. I knew something had to change. It was time to bridle my tongue from the negative and debilitating words I was speaking. It was also time to put into practice my own motto and swallow those words that were not worth saying. In that moment of clarity, I made a conscious choice. Scripture reminds us:

> A wise man's heart guides his mouth, and his lips promote instruction. Pleasant words are a honeycomb, sweet to the soul and healing to the bones. (Proverbs 16:23-24).

I decided I too needed such a wisdom-filled heart that would guide and protect my speech so that my words would be sweet and healing, both physically and spiritually. From that point forward, I began to speak healing, not just to my bones, but my entire body. I started to speak words of fruitfulness and abundance over every area of my life. I also chose to live each day according to the following wisdom given to us by King Solomon:

> My son [daughter], pay attention to what I say; listen closely to my words. Do not let them out of your sight, keep them within your heart; for they are life to those who find them and health to a man's [woman's] whole body. Above all else, guard your heart, for it is the wellspring of life. Put away perversity from your mouth; keep corrupt talk from your lips. (Proverbs 4:20-24)

As King Solomon instructs in this passage, I began to embed God's Word into my heart and daily life. In doing so, I received much-needed hope and confidence throughout my healing journey. And as I gained assurance through reading God's life-giving manual, I was able to replace my habit of speaking negativity and uncertainty with words of blessing and fruitfulness instead. The Bible tells us in John

8:32: "The truth will set you free." By saturating myself in God's word, I received fully his freedom.

Note that in the second part of the above passage, King Solomon entreats us to first safeguard our hearts, then to put away perversity and corrupt talk. I find it significant that King Solomon emphasizes protecting our heart before he mentions taking control of the words we speak. This is because the heart is the center of our emotional well-being and therefore responsible for the words we speak as Jesus himself confirms:

> The mouth speaks what the heart is full of. A good man brings good things out of the good stored up in him, and an evil man brings evil things out of the evil stored up in him. (Matthew 12:34b-35)

> But the things that come out of a person's mouth come from the heart . . . For out of the heart

come evil thoughts [or good ones; my emphasis].

(Matthew 15:18-19)

During the time period when I spoke negatively about my reproductive system, my heart was in a poor condition. I was angry, bitter, and resentful for the suffering I was experiencing. Each of these emotions stemmed from a sick heart and was paralleled in the negative words I uttered.

Once I had a change of heart, I began to trust and believe in the positive words of the Bible. What then began coming out of my mouth mirrored a heart that was hope-filled, faithful, and life-bearing. Whatever the state of my heart was reflected in my speech. So to preserve what came out of my mouth and keep my language clean, I needed first and foremost to safeguard my heart. I also came to learn that the condition of our heart can affect our physical bodies as well:

A heart at peace gives life to the body, but envy
rots the bones. (Proverbs 14:30)

A cheerful heart is good medicine, but a crushed
spirit dries up the bones. (Proverbs 17:22)

These proverbs described well my infertility experience. While my heart was in a poor state, my words were echoing negative sentiments. I believe this negativity had an adverse effect on my menstrual cycle, which at the time ranged anywhere from 30-70 days. Ovulation was all over the place, making it extremely difficult to plan for a pregnancy. The long cycles also gave false hope of a positive result. In conjunction with irregular menstrual cycles, I continued to endure enormous pain, which in turn triggered ongoing negativity towards my womanhood.

From the moment I was convicted of my unbridled tongue in 2002, I repented wholeheartedly of the destructive language I'd been using to speak about my reproductive system. With this change of heart, I went on to replace all negativity with positive statements affirmed by God's Word. I saw immediate physical results. My menstrual cycles shifted to perfect 28-30 day cycles every month. I also had the unusual but very effective gift given to me during this same period whereby I could literally feel the release of my egg (s) during ovulation each month, which helped identify when I was most fertile.

I didn't receive complete healing for the pain I experienced during menstruation until after I became pregnant. But well before then, I made a declaration that I would no longer allow my physical suffering to impact how I spoke about my body. I chose to safeguard once and for all both my heart and my speech, and this in turn greatly blessed my body.

One specific aid I found of benefit during this time of rectifying how I spoke about my womanhood was writing out and confessing two prayers (examples of which

I have included in Appendix III). The apostle Paul reminds us:

> That if you confess with your mouth, Jesus is Lord, and believe in your heart that God raised Him from the dead, you will be saved. For it is with your heart that you believe and are justified, and it is with your mouth that you confess and are saved. (Romans 10:9-10)

This same principle, I felt, applied to my own situation. With a greatly changed heart, I decided to confess the negative words and false impressions I'd held and spoken concerning my female body and fertility status. Through this prayer of confession, I asked God to reveal any words, actions, thought patterns, and belief systems that had bound me to believe contrary to his word. I was then able to acknowledge my wrongdoings and accept God's forgiveness.

Following that initial prayer, I then moved into a time of thanksgiving, praising and thanking God for making me a woman and for the gift of motherhood. I used biblical words and phrases that spoke of fruitfulness (see Appendix II), and I declared health and vitality over my womb, replacing the negative lies I had habitually spoken over my fertility status with life-producing words instead.

The reason I've included in this book an example of these two prayers is twofold. First, I have added them because they form part of my testimony and the healing process I underwent. But their inclusion is also to offer you as reader a tangible aid should you feel led by the Spirit of God to do something similar. I found it extremely beneficial to read books and material that offered something specific to help me on my healing path. So I offer these prayers in the same spirit.

My manner of speech in the early years of my barrenness journey reflected a sick heart. I had no idea my words could keep me bound in such a way that my reproductive system would become affected. An old saying states, "You are what you eat." I think it could read just as accurately, "You are what you say." In fact, I've learned that our words can hold both life and death:

The tongue has the power of life and death, and

those who love it will eat its fruit. Proverbs 18:21

But through God's Word, my sick heart was nursed back to health, and through a now-protected heart, the words I spoke were also safeguarded. I had at last learned to follow the good advice I'd thrown at Jamie all those years ago and swallow what was not worth saying. And as I also learned to safeguard my heart and in consequence my tongue, my entire life became abundantly more fruitful.

The next chapter marks the end of my season of discovery. It describes a four-month intensive worship season whereby I was led to pray, fast, and sing songs of praise as I waited at God's door for his deliverance and the healing touch of his Son, Jesus. Though I didn't know it then, that four-month period marked the final months of my nine-year barrenness journey, segueing into my moment of redemption.

CHAPTER ELEVEN:

God's Wake-Up Call

"Ascribe to the Lord, O mighty ones, ascribe to the Lord Glory and strength. Ascribe to the Lord the glory due His name; worship the Lord in the splendor of His holiness."

— Psalm 29:1-2

The above scripture was given to me by my mentors and friends Bob and Jan Osborne in August, 2005. I confess my initial disappointment when I received this scripture as I was hoping for a more prophetic message like "Nicole, you are healed and the Lord has opened your womb!" But what did eventuate out of this prophetic word was a new and gloriously intimate season of worship that shifted my attention from the inadequacies of my circumstances to focus and accredit glory to God instead.

The month that introduced this new season in my life also marked ten years of marriage for Jamie and me as well as our eighth year of struggling with infertility. Early one Friday morning in August, 2005, I was abruptly roused from slumber by what I can only describe as a wake-up call from God.

During the prior week, I had been pondering the prophetic word my mentors had given me, but I was struggling to understand its significance to my circumstances. Ascribing glory to God and worshipping him in the splendor of his holiness all sounded lovely, but it didn't seem particularly relevant or even helpful to my current status of barrenness.

However, having been unexpectedly awakened on this cold winter's morning, I stirred from my slumber feeling a fervent desire to pray. This was no ordinary impulse to prayer, but something much more raw and passionate. Maybe even words like *bold* and *confident* would describe my desire to pray that morning, much as the writer of the New Testament of Hebrews describes:

> Let us then approach God's throne of grace with confidence, so that we may receive mercy and find grace to help us in our time of need. (Hebrews 4:16)

In that instant, I felt like I was entering into a very significant game-changer moment. And sure enough, as I entered into this anointed time of prayer, something else unfolded. I received a vision of sorts. Now I've already shared with you a number of visions I've experienced over the years, although these were mostly in dreams rather than in a pictorial state. But on this particular morning, the vision I received was quite vivid, and I can only describe it as similar to watching a scene in a movie.

In the vision, I was inside a court room where as the defendant I was seeking resolution for my barren condition. In front of me sat the judge, and my attorney stood between the two of us. Ordinarily it would be the defense counsel's responsibility to speak on the defendant's behalf. But in this case my attorney was allowing me to appeal my own case before the judge.

I rose to my feet, ready to plead my case. Just as with Hannah's game-changer moment, I too had a declaration prepared. During my opening statement, a boldness and confidence came over me as I spoke of my kinship to the King and the inheritance that comes with being the King's daughter. I reminded the judge of biblical scriptures that spoke of God's design for mankind to procreate. I appealed to the judge to grant mercy to me on these grounds and redeem me from my affliction.

Finally, I uttered one name which visibly altered the judge's perspective. I spoke of the redeeming blood of Jesus and claimed his perfect righteousness over my life. Every word I spoke in my court scene vision that morning seemed to evoke love and mercy from the judge. But only one name impacted his justice and secured my freedom—the name of Jesus Christ!

Christ's blood sacrifice, righteousness, and perfection enabled the judge to see me as blameless and righteous too. Through this vision God showed me the true meaning of grace that comes through our Advocate and Redeemer. Jesus, depicted as my attorney in my vision, was advocating for me all along, ready to proclaim me righteous before the judge (God) even if I had not proclaimed it in that moment for myself. My believing in the name of Jesus was enough. His righteousness would cover the rest.

Although I didn't know it at the time, and it wasn't until the end of August that it really became clear (as I will explain shortly), I needed this courtroom vision. You see, even at this late hour with months only remaining until my full healing, the byproduct of a legalistic, faith-by-works church upbringing was still rearing its ugly head, leaving me still striving for results and failing to fully comprehend all Christ has done for us.

There was also a correlation between this courtroom vision and the prophetic word I had already been given, which became clearer by the end of that month. But what happened immediately through these two prophetic experiences was that I entered into a new season in my life. God's wake-up call marked the beginning of a four-month period of intimate praise and worship that altered forever my relationship with the Trinity of God. From that day forward, I dedicated every Friday until I was no longer barren to pray, fast, and to "ascribe to the Lord the glory due his name" and "worship the Lord in the splendor of his holiness" (Psalm 29:2).

The moment I began my Friday Fast days God stirred something deeper within my heart. So often in the past, the focal point had been all about me and the suffering I was experiencing. But when I finally shifted the spotlight away from my shortfalls and onto the beauty of my Creator, all my inadequacies became trivial. When I spent time glorifying God in a worshipful state, basking in his presence, loving and adoring him because he alone is good, any pain I felt was quickly supplanted by his unfailing love.

It was during these final four months of my barrenness journey that Jesus became even more treasured to me and his sacrificial role became more pronounced. Throughout the first half of August, I experienced multiple dreams that all focused on the new blood covenant of Jesus and which tied back into the courtroom vision I had received.

As evidenced in the courtroom vision, some of my former legalistic, faith-by-works mindset was clearly still present in my life and heart as I was sent dream after dream pointing to Christ's sacrifice once and for all. While I'd begun fulfilling the prophetic word I'd received by spending time in close intimacy with my heavenly Father and ascribing him glory, God also wanted me to fully understand and apply the courtroom vision as well.

So for four nights in mid-August 2005, a number of very significant words entered my dreams. Similar to the dream I shared earlier of my search for the heir of the estate, these dreams had an otherworldly feel about them. And I can't come close to describing the wonderful feeling I received through these dreams. Each dream seemed complete and perfect.

The words I kept receiving and the dreams built around these words included the blood of Christ, the cross, the New Covenant, promises, and chapters 9-10 of the New Testament epistle to the Hebrews. One such dream on the second night instigated an immediate Bible study on its contents. The dream was quite simple and brief, consisting of my being handed a love letter in the form of an ancient scroll. When I opened the scroll, the letter consisted of passages from the book of Hebrews referencing promises and a New Covenant.

Prior to this dream, I had spent little if any time reading the book of Hebrews. But during that month of August, 2005, Hebrews became everything to me. I came to truly accept that Christ came as our High Priest and went through the greater and more perfect tabernacle (chapter 9) and that his sacrifice is once and for all (chapter 10).

Numerous dreams I received during the month of August pointed to one thing. Jesus is my Redeemer. There once was a covenant that required something from us, but not anymore. Jesus has done it all, fulfilling the old covenant and making way for the new.

My Friday Fast days became a prelude into the sequence of dreams I received that month. The more time I spent in intimacy with God, the more he revealed. I can truly say that every Friday was the one day of the week I looked forward to the most. I learned so much about my Savior God during this intimate season, and I established a deep love for the Holy Spirit as well. I also came to appreciate worship as never before. Entering into the Throne Room of Grace and basking in my Father's love and affection became the most sacred and precious time of my life.

When I finally conceived and my daughter was soon to be born, I remember spending one last interlude in this precious, intimate space before my God. It had been over a year since first I began dedicating every Friday in this manner. And although I no longer fasted since I was now eating for two, I nevertheless remained dedicated to this intimate time with my Father.

This particular day just prior to my daughter's birth stands out as one of my most sacred. I was worshipping and singing praises to my wonderful Father, glorifying the King of Kings and Lord of Lords, just dancing and enjoying intimacy with God when I sensed tears rolling down his face.

As tears spilled down my own cheeks in response to his, I asked my loving Father why he was crying.

His reply was so incredibly touching and unbelievably humbling to me. The great, almighty God of the universe was exceedingly happy that he could gift me, his daughter, with the desires of my heart—children. But his gift to me also meant that our time together was going to change. While my heart would always be devoted to loving him, God knew the reality of motherhood meant my devotion would no longer be solely his. From then on, it would be shared with my offspring, and this pained and grieved my Abba Father.

Intimacy with God is what my mentors' prophetic word initiated. Coupled with the courtroom vision as well as the numerous "New Covenant" dreams, I came to see that these prophetic experiences were completely intertwined. The more time I spent ascribing glory to God and worshipping him in the splendor of his holiness, the more I comprehended the sacrificial role and amazing grace of my Redeemer Jesus

Christ. As I focused on the beauty of my wonderful Savior, he became everything and my shortcomings diminished.

During this season, I found myself surrendering, submitting, and accepting that God alone is perfect, that his will would be done, and that I need only to trust in him. With Jesus's righteousness covering me, I no longer needed to strive in the natural. I could simply glorify his name, and that was enough!

Although I had desired a more straightforward and immediate deliverance-type prophetic word from my mentor friends, I will be forever grateful for the word I received instead. Intimacy with God has defined my Christian walk from that first breathtaking Friday Fast day to the present. I still dedicate time during my week to just be still, worshipping and praising my loving Father, listening and basking in his glorious Throne Room. What started off as a discipline, dedicating one day per week, has developed into a relational experience I cannot do without. My relationship with my heavenly Father, the Son, and the Holy Spirit is by far the greatest gift I received out of my painful barrenness journey, and I will be eternally grateful for it.

The next and last section of *Having Faith* details my final months as a barren woman, followed by my new life as a mum. It is the glorious ending to my long nine-year journey in the wilderness. Numerous breakthroughs occurred during my last four months as a barren woman, especially during the month of October. The next chapter marks my ascent out of infertility and into motherhood. It highlights the faithfulness of my loving Father in heaven. And it celebrates his perfect redemption plan for my life.

PART THREE:

It Is Finished

CHAPTER TWELVE:

October Rainbows

"The Lord has taken away your punishment; he has turned back your enemy. He will take great delight in you, He will quiet you with His love, He will rejoice over you with singing."

— Zephaniah 13:17

Rainbows have always been my favorite natural phenomenon. I am transfixed by their beauty and can gaze at their arc of colors for hours. I love their spiritual connotation as well—a covenant promise of God's everlasting faithfulness and mercy to mankind (Genesis 9:3). Each time I am witness to a rainbow, I sense the depth of God's love for his children and I am overcome with gratitude and awe. So it in no way surprises me that God would choose to speak to me during my final months of barrenness through my most beloved natural marvel.

Throughout October, 2005, rainbows became increasingly significant to my journey. During this same time period, a scripture passage from Isaiah 54 spoke very clearly to me and became interwoven with this theme of rainbows:

> Sing, barren woman, you who never bore a child; burst into song, shout for joy, you who were never in labour . . . Do not be afraid; you will not be put to shame. Do not fear disgrace; you will not be humiliated. You will forget the shame of your youth and remember no more the reproach of your widowhood. For your Maker is your husband—the Lord Almighty is his name—the Holy One of Israel is your Redeemer; he is called the God of all the earth . . . For a brief moment I abandoned you, but with deep compassion I will bring you back. In a surge of anger I hid my face

from you for a moment, but with everlasting kindness I will have compassion on you, says the Lord your Redeemer. To me this is like the days of Noah, when I swore that the waters of Noah would never again cover the earth. So now I have sworn not to be angry with you, never to rebuke you again . . . All your children will be taught by the Lord, and great will be their peace . . . This is the heritage of the servants of the Lord, and this is their vindication from me, declares the Lord. (Isaiah 54:1-17)

This stunning passage of Scripture became my go-to reading for most of October. I couldn't stop studying and pondering it. It described my barrenness journey perfectly, almost disturbingly so. From my early years of feeling ashamed, rejected, and even believing that I was being rebuked and punished by God, Isaiah 54 detailed my troubles precisely.

But thankfully, Isaiah 54 doesn't finish with retribution and damnation, and neither does my story. Just as the prophet Isaiah describes, it was with everlasting kindness and compassion that God drew me back to himself, forgetting my past and replacing all my shame and guilt with a promise of restoration, deliverance, freedom, and vindication. And similar also to Isaiah's picture of a barren woman who was instructed to sing and shout for joy, I too felt the need to supplant a grief-stricken heart with songs of praise and shouts of acclamation to my Redeemer, which had begun two months earlier on my Friday Fast days.

But apart from this amazing restoration that God was doing in my life, there was something else in Isaiah 54 that caught my attention—a reference to the covenant promise made by God to Noah (v. 9). A promise of God's faithfulness and love to all of mankind that God had confirmed with the covenant sign of a rainbow. The same rainbow that had become a sort of a covenant sign to me as well.

This began during the first two weeks of October, 2005, when I became witness to daily sightings of rainbows. The forecast didn't seem to matter. Whether raining, overcast, or sunny, I still saw at least one rainbow every day. Yes, this could have been an astonishing coincidence. But to me, God was giving me a symbol of hope. Much needed hope! My October rainbows signaled to me that my days of barrenness were coming to an end and the Promised Land of children was drawing ever closer.

Other momentous breakthroughs occurred as well during October that were a prelude to my hour of deliverance. In this chapter, my aim is to give you a glimpse of what God was doing in my life at that time. Some of what I share may seem fantastical to you. Wake-up calls from God, dreams and visions, and now daily rainbow viewings may already fit into that category. But since this is the conclusion of my healing story, I hope you will bear with my testimony and accept that God does move at times in mysterious ways.

I would also like to preface this chapter with a disclaimer. I am not anyone special. I don't have some secret method to gain the attention of our loving Father. Remember I was in the wilderness for nine years before my deliverance arrived, proof that I am not more favored than any other.

But I will say that through my exhaustive journey I came to know my true identity and my worth in Christ. I am a child of God's, a daughter of the Most High, a princess of the King, created in God's image, loved and adored despite my failings, pronounced righteous because of the righteousness of my Savior.

Just as I can speak with my earthly dad at any time, my true identity as a member of God's family gives me constant access to my Father in heaven. That truth is what helped me forge an intimate relationship with God. And it is due to that forged bond that I sought to be included in God's plans for my life. In consequence, my eyes and my ears were always well inclined to receive whatever communication God wanted to impart to me. And this can be true for any one of God's children. It is not exclusive to me.

The other thing I really came to understand is that God was pursuing me all along. I certainly didn't embrace his pursuit of me in my early years of marriage. Quite the opposite! But just as any good earthly parent won't give up on their children despite their shortcomings, my rejection of God did not prevent his steadfast pursuit of me. In fact, he may have pressed in even harder as any good parent would.

The strange rainbow phenomenon that began my three-month ascent out of barrenness and into motherhood started on October 1st, 2005. This daily rainbow viewing lasted about a fortnight. I'm sure that first rainbow sighting was as beautiful as any, bringing a much-needed smile to my face and reminding me of the beauty that is my Creator. But in truth I don't remember it specifically. It was just one more stunning but typical rainbow, so I didn't give it much thought at all.

It wasn't until some days later that I started to recognize the peculiarity of what I was seeing. The occasional rainbow viewing is normal and natural, but seeing them daily, sometimes multiple sightings throughout the day, seemed extraordinary. After a few days of seeing rainbows, my radar picked up and I started to take notice.

But it wasn't rainbows that initially made October 1st, 2005, memorable for me. What sets the background, ushering in a month of breakthroughs, is actually a dream I had that night. The October 1st dream superseded another dream I had received earlier that year. The dream depicted a dam that was completely empty and dry. At the bottom of the dam was a lock, firmly shut, preventing any water from pouring in and filling the catchment.

This first dream seemed to correspond with the vision I've already shared of a lock firmly sealed over my womb for which we'd eventually sought prayer healing. The October 1st dream depicted the same dam, but instead of being barren and locked, the dam wall had broken loose and water was gushing in, filling the dam completely.

I saw this second dream as a fulfillment of the first. After my Friday Fast days of basking in God's presence and experiencing intimacy with the Holy Spirit, the second dream with water gushing in seemed to illustrate the outpouring of God's love I was now experiencing. And where the dry, empty dam represented a barren, unfruitful womb sealed by a lock, this second dream depicted a fruitfulness that was the outgrowth of the Holy Spirit overflowing in my life.

The second dream also included no hint of a lock. This I consider a reflection of my newfound understanding of Jesus, who had become so central to my Friday Fast days, especially with the many dreams that pointed to his sacrifice once and for all. Jesus always held the key to my fruitfulness, and so I have absolute assurance it was he who unlocked my womb, typified in the second dream as a dam now open and overflowing.

I mention these two dreams partly from a sequential reference point, but also because they represent a before and after picture of my spiritual walk with the Trinity of God. Where the first dream was fruitless and barren, the second was teeming with abundance, a pictorial vision of what God was doing in my life.

You see, my relationship with God was integral for the healing of my womb. This may not be the case for every woman going through a barrenness experience. But I do know it was central to the overall healing God was doing in my own life. I was being restored in every area of my life, and barrenness was the last piece of restoration that needed to be healed.

After I had this dream, the following two weeks continued with the phenomenal visions of rainbows. Every day, on some days multiple times, I would feast my eyes upon arcs of color. I found myself in a permanent state of amazement, looking to God for his understanding on what I was seeing, drawn to him like never before, thankful for the gift he was offering me.

I spent much time in worship and prayer during this period. I had begun to see that I was entering a game-changer moment, and I didn't want to miss anything. I desperately sought to understand what was happening, and I greatly wanted answers. I sensed that perhaps it was time to go back for prayer healing with the prayer team I had seen earlier for the lock over my womb. But I was reluctant to go without God's full blessing. Although I saw the rainbow viewings as a sign of healing to come, I still needed a precise message, a defining moment that spoke of God's approval.

On October 17th, a few days after my last rainbow viewing, I received my answer. I was in church listening to my pastor preach on the biblical character Joseph. The pastor was highlighting the long-awaited fulfillment of Joseph's childhood prophetic dreams. Even though these had encountered a long delay, they were nevertheless eventually fulfilled.

This message of completion and the fact that it spoke of a long-drawn-out fulfillment process really spoke to me. I sensed God was inviting me, even urging me, to be prayed for that morning. So during the altar call at the end of the service, I made my way down to the front, ready and waiting to be prayed for.

This wasn't something I was accustomed to doing since my original return to church when my disobedient legs had carried me forward for prayer. But on this particular day, I felt very convicted to answer the call. To my surprise, a woman with the same name as my biblical role model, Ruth, asked to pray for me. Ruth's prayer that morning was very simple, but it was exactly the right prayer for me. All she requested was that a door be opened and that God show me the right person to pray for the healing of my womb.

While I would certainly have preferred a word of healing, Ruth's prayer that day was incredibly prophetic for two reasons. First, as I've mentioned several times already, I had received a prophetic picture of a door firmly sealed over my womb, which Ruth could not have known about. For her to pray that a door be opened was very significant and anointed.

Secondly, Ruth's prayer that I be guided to the right person to pray for me coincided with what I had been asking God to reveal to me during the first two weeks of

October. As I stated before, I had wanted to go back to the people who had prayed for the lock over my womb to be released. But I was waiting for confirmation from God for this as I didn't want to go without his authority. Ruth's prayer didn't exactly confirm this. However, a dream I had that night most definitely did.

In my dream, Jamie and I were in a basement surrounded by rainbows. I saw visions of rainbows everywhere, and I was holding two rainbows, one in each hand. I sensed in the dream that the rainbows I held represented my future children and the surrounding rainbows signified a new and wonderful covenant between Jesus and me. Water was gushing into the basement where we were standing, and yet I was not afraid. In fact, I was excited as I sensed it was a flooding of the Holy Spirit.

The dream had an end-of-an-era feeling to it as though it was a completion of a season. Before the dream ended, God gave me one final instruction, the directive I had been hoping for throughout that month. God not only gave me his blessing, but he bid me to go back for prayer to the church group that had previously prayed for the unlocking of my womb.

This was a hugely exciting moment for me. I had been praying and seeking God for this release for many weeks. I had learned that to move separately from God's will for my life only took me on another lap around the mountain, so I was not at all prepared to go anywhere without his complete directive and authority. To receive a dream that explicitly named who would pray for my healing was unbelievably exhilarating.

October 30th, 2005, was a day that changed Jamie's and my lives forever. That was the day we finally arrived at the church service where God had directed me to receive prayer for deliverance. But during the lead-up to this momentous milestone, I still faced numerous obstacles that almost prevented my receiving the healing I sought.

I experienced a number of spiritual attacks, including a week-long debilitating virus that lasted all the way to the day of the church service. I remember feeling so sick when we left for the service that Jamie had to help me to the car. I had only felt this way one other time. Significantly, that was the day Jamie and I rededicated our marriage.

But that in itself was an encouragement as we'd sensed on the prior occasion that my sickness was a spiritual assault to prevent our renewing our marriage vows. We knew how much the enemy hated the idea of Jamie and I recommitting our marriage with God front and center at the helm of our union. And we knew full well that the devil would also hate to see us establish a godly family. So this second sickness I faced on October 30th only strengthened my resolve. Nothing was going to keep me from attending that church service.

Even once we arrived, the enemy still tried hard to prevent me from receiving the healing God wanted to provide. At this specific service, almost everyone had come for one reason only—to request prayer. Before I could even leave my seat at the end of the service, the pastor I'd been instructed in my dream to approach was overwhelmed with prayer requests. The line to meet with her was nearly out the door. And since the pastor spent quality time with each person, the resultant wait was a long one.

As I was still feeling very unwell, I decided to remain in my seat until the crowd diminished before joining the long line of parishioners seeking prayer. I can't even describe how impatient I felt at that moment. I had waited nine years for this day, and I knew I was on a God-mission, not just a Nicole-mission.

Finally, after everyone else had been ministered to, my turn came. But just as the pastor greeted me, the hall lights were turned off and everyone was asked to leave the building. It was like one last straw of Satan's relentless attacks against me that day. I remember feeling like the woman with the issue of blood mentioned in the gospels (Mark 5:25-34). The woman knew she could be healed if she could just touch the hem of Jesus's tunic. I too was resolute in my belief that I was going to be healed this day. All I needed was a prayer from the person I'd been instructed by God to see.

The pastor apologetically informed me that we needed to vacate the hall. But when she added that I should schedule an appointment for a pastoral meeting with her office (at that time a five-month waiting list!), a boldness came over me as I'd never experienced before. Just like the woman who'd doggedly pushed her way through the crowd to reach Jesus, I too believed Jesus was my only answer for healing, and no obstacle was going to stop me from touching my Savior's cloak. If I hadn't allowed sickness to prevent my attendance, I was certainly not going to leave that church building without completing my mission.

I am not naturally a forthright kind of a person. But on that evening I forcefully and tenaciously made my intentions known, refusing to leave without being prayed for. And I was prayed for, dimmed lights and all. After all, how could the pastor refuse such steadfast resolve!

God revealed to this pastor every spiritual blockage that prevented Jamie and me from conceiving. Much of what she saw, I had already been shown through dreams and visions. One such blockage was the exact same medical diagnosis we'd received years earlier—that there was hardness over my eggs preventing Jamie's sperm from penetrating through. Where the doctors had explained it as some unknown physical phenomenon, the pastor saw the spiritual reason behind it and released it in Jesus's name.

Each blockage that was identified was removed through prayer in the name of Jesus. This was no big exhibition, just quiet and calm. The power came through the mighty name of Jesus Christ. His authority alone released me from bondage and ultimately produced healing and freedom.

I'm not sure why this person was given the ability to pray for my release when much of what she spoke of I had already identified and prayed about myself. But God uses the gifts of many to his glory, and I have no doubt my healing would in turn increase this woman's faith in God to use her in a mighty healing ministry.

At the end of the prayer, the pastor received a vision and proclaimed: "I see a door open!"

I cannot describe what those words meant to me. For so long Jamie and I had lived with a pictorial image of a door firmly shut over my womb that was keeping us bound. But at that very moment when this pastor said she saw a door open, I knew it was finished. Tears streamed down my face. I could scarcely draw breath. It was done. I was

healed. I had been delivered, and I was going to be a mum!

CHAPTER THIRTEEN:

Happily Ever After Ending

" He settles the barren woman in her home, as a happy mother of children. Praise the Lord." — Psalm 113:9

The conception of our daughter Faith took place just shy of two months after my prayer/healing experience. Those weeks were a real challenge for me. I had expected to fall pregnant effortlessly and promptly as soon as I left the church that evening of October 30th. I really thought my mission was finished, my faith appointment complete. But God's timing is not our timing, and to accomplish his perfect will, he had one final assignment for me.

That assignment was to tell people, wherever I went and to whomever I spoke, that God had performed a miracle of healing and I would soon become pregnant. I was not given a timeframe for when I would conceive, so this task seemed a daunting one. Just how long would I have to proclaim my upcoming pregnancy? Days? Months? Even years?

But by this stage of my journey, I had learned to be obedient no matter the cost. So everywhere I went throughout the remaining two months of 2005, I did announce my pending pregnancy, giving glory to my Father in heaven. We were invited to attend a number of large outings during those two months, including many friends we hadn't seen for quite a long time. This meant proclaiming my good news to a lot of people. Their reaction was mostly awkward nervousness as well as pity. They clearly felt my nine-year journey had blinded me to the obvious, which was that it was time for me to let go of a dream no one else believed would happen.

And I did feel somewhat foolish openly and publicly declaring that God would shortly deliver our miracle. In retrospect, I can see why God wanted me to make this very public confession. God knew that through my confession people would witness firsthand God's faithfulness to his promises once what I professed came to pass.

And that is exactly what happened. The conception of my firstborn Faith took place at God's appointed time less than two months from the day the door to my womb was opened. I cannot even describe how Jamie and I felt the morning we found out we were expecting a child. It may be hard for those who haven't gone through infertility to identify with nine years of negative results. Basically, it equates to 108 menstrual cycles, 3285 days of desperate longing.

So words simply cannot do justice to the emotion we experienced as we read that positive result on the pregnancy test. Today I have three children who are each the product of God's perfect timing, and so I am forever grateful that God chose the timing exactly when he did.

In truth, there was nothing unusual about the month when we finally conceived. I had no intuition nor received any sign that this month was going to be any different than the last. I can even remember crying out to God in late December, 2005, asking him through a torrent of tears, "How do I know that I will actually conceive?"

I think even God's boundless patience must have been running low by then. His answer to my tearful plea was simple but stern: "Because I gave you my Word!"

This hit me right between the eyes. God's answer also held a double meaning. Even at this late stage, I was still questioning God's faithfulness, still struggling to trust, still anxious whether the miracle I'd been proclaiming to everyone would actually come true. Through this simple statement, God reminded me that not only has he given me his written Word, the Bible, which cannot lie, but that I should know by this point in my long journey with him that God is always true to his word.

What I didn't know as I bowed my head to God's gentle reprimand was that I was already pregnant. Sunday, January 22nd, 2006 was my dad's 56th birthday. Jamie had felt a conviction for at least a week at this juncture that I was pregnant and was urging me daily to take a pregnancy test. In fact, he was so certain that he'd purchased multiple over-the-counter pregnancy tests for me, something he had never done before.

But I resisted, gripped with fear of another failed cycle. After all, what was the likely chance of this month being different than all the rest? Yes, my menstrual cycle was past due, but could I be sure the wild fluctuations of the past years were really over?

Finally, on Sunday, January 22nd, I surrendered to Jamie's pleading. Still convinced it was pointless, I stubbornly remained in bed, allowing Jamie to read the results first. He stood quietly with his back to me, remaining motionless for so long that every fear and anxiety I'd ever felt surfaced. Surely his stillness signaled another month of shattered dreams.

I was convinced this was the case, and I felt I just couldn't bear it any longer. So many negative emotions filled me at that moment. I wanted something to swallow me up so I would never have to face life again. Doubt and disbelief raged through me in one final, mighty burst. Thoughts of humiliation raced through my head. I felt I'd yet again failed my husband. And that I'd also let God down. The mission he'd given me must still be incomplete.

How this pity-party of mine must have grieved my loving Father! At the very moment he was delivering my long-awaited gift of motherhood, all I could do was disbelieve.

Then Jamie swung around to face me. He looked stunned, overcome with emotion, even awed. He tried to speak, but no words came out. Finally, he got out a single short phrase, just four wonderful words: "Nik, you are pregnant!"

I wish I had greater skill as a writer to convey that moment in time. All I can say is that the instant Jamie said those words my pulse began racing a million miles per hour. Okay, maybe not literally, but I could barely breathe.

Jumping out of bed, I scanned the pregnancy test for myself, unable to believe it could really be true. I even conducted a second test, all the while rebuking my husband for most likely doing it wrong (sorry darling!). Immediately, another positive result appeared. It was true. I was pregnant. I was not *going* to be a mum. I was NOW a mum!

The next ten minutes or so went something like this. I fell to the ground in a fit of laughter. This outburst of hilarity brought Jamie to the floor beside me. Together, we gave way to our glee in a state of sheer ecstasy. We laughed and laughed, unable to stop. It was as though the previous nine years of brokenness had been supplanted by pure joy that burst from us beyond our control.

The joy engulfing us was the perfect ending to the longest, most intense season of our lives. From there, we had the absolute privilege and honor to share the good news of what our Father had done for us with all our family and friends. Ultimately, it was God who was exalted, glorified, and lifted up high, for he alone held the key to our fruitfulness.

For the next eight months, I had the sheer joy of carrying and nurturing within my womb my sweet Faith Crystal. What a gift she was then and remains to this day. Then in 2008 and again in 2010, I was given the added blessing of bearing two sons, Joel Samuel and Levi James.

God answered our prayers and gave us the desires of our heart—two sons and a daughter. How then can my heart be turned to anything but my Father all the days of my life?

He has given me everything I have asked for and so much more!

And even if I hadn't receive what I thought I wanted, I know God would have had something even more perfect planned for my life because he alone is good and his will is flawless. All I need do is trust in him.

My barrenness years were exhausting, complex, and took me on a unique pathway. But out of that extraordinary experience, my life was transformed. I became the woman I am today because of the faith journey I went through. *Having Faith* was not something for which I was prepared, but rather something for which God had been equipping me during nine long years.

Out of a painful barrenness journey, Jesus became my Conqueror, my Deliverer, my Redeemer, the Lover of my soul, my Friend, my Savior, my Overcomer, my Everything.

And as I walked this arduous journey, the Holy Spirit became my Guidance Counsellor, the Wisdom behind everything I do. He is the One I walk and talk with in the cool of the day. He is the God who fills my heart with so much love and joy that I am bursting with his grace.

And my Abba Father, to whom this journey is truly dedicated, I thank you one-thousand times over, for gifting your daughter with more than I could ever hope for. Thank you, Lord over my life. I truly and deeply am in love with you!

CHAPTER FOURTEEN:

My Love Story

"My Beloved is mine and I am his."
– Song of Solomon 2:16a

———————⁓———————

Without a doubt, my barrenness to motherhood journey is my very own love story. It is the tale of an ordinary Aussie girl with an extraordinary Father in heaven. The script is a classic romance-drama starring a rebellious young lady seeking to control her own destiny. But when her life spirals out of control, she becomes lost and confused, overwhelmed by her own choices.

Meanwhile, her family is searching for her. Her Father and his Son are relentless in their pursuit even as she rejects their advances, never giving up on her, always

269

opening doors and inviting her in. Though whispers calling her home reach her ears, feelings of worthlessness holds her back.

But eventually her family's tender compassion and forgiveness break down the rebellious young lady's defiant resistance. Truth and light illuminate her deepest pains, filling her instead with hope and joy. When her Father holds out his wide-open arms to her, she runs straight into the full embrace of one who loves like no other. Finally, she is home where she belongs, and finally she can begin to heal.

This story is my own, and although for some it may sound like a melodrama, to me it is the ultimate love story of a Father rescuing and saving one of his daughters. I didn't really deserve all I received from my heavenly Father. But then again, nobody does. It is by the grace of Jesus alone that I am a mother today. It is his faithfulness, his unselfish, unconditional love that fulfilled my every need, my every desire.

I hope my love story has been a source of inspiration to you. Although what I've shared is my own unique experience, our Father's love is deep and stretches to all his children. I have no doubt that God wants to feature in every one of his children's life stories, including yours. God has a plan and purpose for each of our lives, yours and mine, and he wants to direct us through it. From my experience, when we allow him access, the narrative of our life becomes so much richer and will always result in the perfect *happily-ever-after* ending.

EPILOGUE:

A Whale of a Tale

"But Jonah ran away from the Lord and headed for Tarshish.

He went down to Joppa, where he found a ship bound for that

port. After paying for the fare, he went aboard and sailed for

Tarshish to flee from the Lord."

– Jonah 1:3

At church recently, I experienced a semi-crisis related to worship leading—namely my lack of musical talent! My pastor, Simon, responded to this in a way that both encouraged and challenged me. He pointed out to me that whatever I consider to be my strengths God may, in fact, see as my weaknesses. And whatever I consider to be my weaknesses God may, in fact, see as my strengths.

Perhaps, Simon went on to say, it was through my *considered weaknesses* that God would most use me for his glory. After all, the apostle Paul himself once exulted:

> For Christ's sake, I delight in weaknesses, in insults, in hardships, in persecutions, in difficulties. For when I am weak, then I am strong. (2 Corinthians 12:10)

I found my pastor's words profound and impacting. Certainly, God had used the weaknesses of so many men and women in biblical times to further his Kingdom. Moses came to mind as an amazing spokesman for God despite a speech impediment (Exodus 4:10). David was but a young shepherd boy when he was tasked with slaying a giant (1 Samuel 17). Then there was Esther, a mere Jewish orphan who became a Persian queen and saved her people from annihilation (Esther 1-9).

My musical impairment might not be such as an impediment as these biblical heroes faced. But my weakness as a vocalist was certainly causing me enormous angst at this time of my life. The conundrum I faced was this. I knew I was created to *ascribe greatness to God* and *worship the Lord in the splendour of his holiness* (Psalm 29:1-2) as had been revealed to me during my Friday Fast days many years earlier. I had also been shown by God years prior that he was raising me up to lead worship, something my lack of musical talent made easy for me to dismiss at the time.

Having now been asked to lead worship, I was faced with a real challenge. I might feel God's calling on my life to lead worship, but my vocal abilities could be described as "back-up singer" at best. Every doubt and insecurity I had about myself overcame me. After leading a few times, I became paralysed with fear. I wanted to run and hide all at the same time. I begged God to release me from this ministry. I started to doubt my earlier conviction that this was at all my calling.

–Having Faith–

I was in such turmoil, angry at God that he would ask me to do a ministry that caused me such angst. Amidst my little tantrum, during one Sunday morning service I refused to worship God. Expressing my deep love and affection to my King always evokes praise and worship from my heart. But on this Sunday morning, I simply gritted my teeth and refused to worship my heavenly Father at all. I knew I was grieving God even as I denied him my affection. And this caused me even greater pain.

That very afternoon, my daughter Faith was playing Teen Fiona in the musical Shrek. As I exuberantly expressed my praise for Faith's performance, clapping loudly, beaming with pride for her achievement, enthusiastic for all she'd accomplished, God whispered gently but clearly in my ear: "How can you lavish esteem on Faith but refuse to extravagantly worship me?"

Wow! How could I indeed? It was the first time since truly knowing my heavenly Father that I had denied him all of myself, especially in worship. But though I was truly repentant and never wanted to deny God my extravagant worship again, I was still desperate to get out of being a worship leader. And I was still prepared to run from God if that meant my release.

A few days later, God once again spoke to me. This time it was through the biblical story of Jonah, who had been given a prophetic word for his people but refused to deliver it, running instead in the opposite direction (Jonah 1:1-2). This was exactly what I too planned on doing. I figured I could praise and worship as needed within the congregation, maybe even sing back-up, but surely that would be enough.

Of course, when Jonah tried this with the mission God gave him, he ended up in the belly of a whale (Jonah 1:17). I was concerned that my own running might end in similar heartache!

–Having Faith–

It was on a family cruise to the South Pacific Islands that God put an end to my little pity-party. I could not resolve my conundrum. Deep inside, I knew what God was asking of me. But my inadequacies screamed in my face, and I couldn't get past my insecurities. In reality, it was most likely my vanity that was taking a hit. If I couldn't sing perfectly, why should I put myself out there in such a public way?

This cloud hanging over me was preventing me from enjoying my family holiday as I ought. I needed answers. I decided that if God truly wanted me as a worship leader in my local church, then I would be the very best I could for him. I would be as vulnerable as he desired me to be. I would embarrass myself, if that's what it took. But I was not going to do it unless I knew categorically that this was God's desire for my life.

So I asked for a sign. Hoping this would put an end to the silly nonsense rattling around in my head, I asked for the impossible. I figured that if I was acting like Jonah, then perhaps I needed my very own whale experience to end it once and for all. I asked God to send a whale and have it jump out of the water that very day as a sign that worship leading was part of my calling.

I was kind of hoping I wouldn't see a whale so as to justify not leading worship ever again. Yet at the same time, I desperately wanted to see one as a symbol of God's amazing love and continued working in my life.

As it turns out, I had my whale encounter within the hour. I'd just settled my three children into their kid's club activities, and Jamie and I were just about to relax in the ship's adult lounge when another guest on the ship yelled, "Whale!"

Sure enough, as we all rushed for a good viewing spot, one single magnificent whale out past the ship's stern jumped out of the water putting to rest once and for all my worship tantrum!

This is just one of many faith encounters I've experienced since my barren years ended. For me, my whale tale highlights my ongoing, deep need to be included in my Father's plan and purpose for my life. I never want to walk a different path from his. I've been there before, and it always results in multiple laps around a mountain. Not to mention, an unsettled and grieved heart.

As I'd promised God, from my whale encounter onward I dedicated myself to the calling he had given me. I am still not completely comfortable in my role as worship leader, but that's my weakness. I trust that God will see my inadequacies as my strength, something he can use to fulfil his glory. After all, it is in our imperfections that we need rely mostly on him. And it is out of that complete reliance that God can bring about beauty from ashes, a joyous blessing from mourning, festive praise instead of despair (Isaiah 61:3).

I hope *Having Faith* has been a source of comfort for you. This faith walk we are on is a lifetime journey for all of us. For Jamie and me, our faith journey did not end at conception, but continues to be refined daily by our Creator. We have learned over the years that where we sow in tears, God brings forth a harvest in his perfect timing. A scripture that describes every faith journey I have encountered in the last decade affirms this beautifully:

> Those who sow in tears will reap with songs of joy. He who goes out weeping, carrying seed to sow, will return with songs of joy, carrying sheaves with him. (Psalm 126:5-6)

And now as I finally put down my pen, I pray God's abundance over your life. I pray that you will know the depth of love our Father has for you. You are his design. You are his favoured daughter or son. You are complete in and through his Son Jesus. May you experience all of him intimately, and may your very own faith journey reflect his perfect plan for your life.

In God's grace and mercy,

~Nicole~

A Blessing from Numbers 6:24-26:

The Lord bless you and keep you;

The Lord make his face shine on

you and be gracious to you;

The Lord turn his face towards you

and give you peace.

APPENDIX ONE:

All the Barren Women of

the Bible

"Blessed is everyone who fears the Lord, who walks in his ways . . . Your wife shall be like a fruitful vine. In the very heart of your house, your children like olive plants all around your table. Behold this shall the man be blessed, who fears the Lord." —Psalm 128:1, 3-4

The Bible mentions by name five women who had difficulty conceiving but eventually received the gift of motherhood. These women were: Sarah, Rebekah, Rachel, Hannah, and Elizabeth, mother of John the Baptist. While Scripture does not specifically state that Ruth was barren, I am including her in this list since she remained childless for at least the ten years before her first husband died. All these women were historically significant because of the offspring they ultimately bore.

In addition to these women, a number of other families were also affected by barrenness. In this appendix, I offer a brief account of each testimony. Since a chapter each has already been devoted to Sarah, Rachel, and Hannah, I have not included their struggles with infertility in this section.

Rebekah

Sarah conceived a child in her nineties and, as instructed by God, named him Isaac. After his mother's death when he was forty years old, Isaac married Rebekah. Isaac and Rebekah remained childless for twenty years before Rebekah conceived twins, Jacob and Esau:

Isaac pleaded with the Lord for his wife, because she was barren; and the Lord granted his plea, and Rebekah conceived . . . Isaac was sixty years old when Rebekah gave birth to them Genesis 25:21, 26)

Ruth

Ruth is famed for her faithful devotion to her mother in-law Naomi (Ruth 2:11; 4:15). But she clearly had fertility difficulties as she was married to her first husband for ten years before he died, but remained childless. After marrying her second husband Boaz, Ruth gave birth to a son named Obed, the father of Jesse, who was in turn the father of David, from whose lineage was ultimately born the Messiah, Jesus Christ.

Elizabeth

The only barren woman mentioned in the New Testament is Elizabeth, mother of John the Baptist.

Elizabeth and her husband Zachariah were well-known for their godly character when an angel appeared to Zachariah to give him the good news of a son:

> Both of them were righteous in the sight of God, observing all the Lord's commands and decrees blamelessly. But they were childless because Elizabeth was not able to conceive, and they were both very old . . . The angel said to him [Zechariah]: 'Do not be afraid, Zechariah; your prayer has been heard. Your wife Elizabeth will bear you a son, and you are to call him John. [14] He will be a joy and delight to you, and many will rejoice because of his birth, [15] for he will be great in the sight of the Lord (Luke1:6-7, 13-15).

Abimelech's Household

Abimelech was a Canaanite ruler who took Sarah as his wife after Abraham had deceived him that Sarah was only his sister. God protected her from Abimelech during her stay in Abimelech's haram, but the wombs of all women in Abimelech's household, including his own wives and concubines, became barren until Sara was released:

> "The Lord had closed up all the wombs of the house of Abimelech, because of Sarah, Abraham's wife. So Abraham prayed to God; and God healed Abimelech, his wife, and his maidservants. Then they bore children. (Genesis 20:17-18)

Manoah's Wife (Samson's mother)

Manoah's wife was another significant mother of the Bible, although her name is not mentioned. She too was barren when an angel of the Lord visited her with the news that she would give birth to one of Israel's most powerful judges, Samson, who would deliver the Israelites from their oppressors, the Philistines:

You are sterile and childless, but you are going to conceive and have a son. Now see to it that you drink no wine or other fermented drink and that you do not eat anything unclean, because you will conceive and give birth to a son. No razor may be used on his head because the boy is to be a Nazirite, set apart to God from birth, and he will begin the deliverance of Israel from the hands of the Philistines. (Judges 13:3-5)

The Shunammite Woman

Another woman who could not conceive is identified only as a Shunammite woman who opened the hospitality of her home to the prophet Elisha (3 Kings 4). In appreciation Elisha prophesied over her that she would bear a son within the year. This woman became pregnant as foretold, and later on her son was raised from the dead by Elisha in response to the faith this remarkable woman had.

Michal

The only biblical account of a woman remaining childless until death was that of Michal, daughter of Saul and first wife of King David. Michal initially loved David (1 Samuel 18:20), but when David was sent into exile, fleeing from her father, she was given in marriage to another man (1 Samuel 25:44). We don't know how long this second marriage lasted, but at least ten years. Nor is there indication she had any children with her second husband.

Sometime after becoming king but before conquering Jerusalem, David demanded Michal be returned to him. Her second husband is described as weeping bitterly when she was taken from him (2 Samuel 3:12-16). We aren't told how Michel herself felt about it, but sometime later when David was bringing the Ark of the Covenant to Jerusalem, Michal saw David dancing in the street and "despised him in her heart" (2 Samuel 6:16). In consequence, Michal had no children to the day of her death" (2 Samuel 6:23), though whether because of barrenness or because David exiled her to his harem isn't clear.

APPENDIX TWO:

Words of Comfort

"Blessed is she who has believed that what the Lord has said to her will be accomplished." —Luke 1:45

There are countless scriptures that increased my faith and offered me comfort throughout my years of barrenness. In this appendix, I include some of my favorites in the hope that God's Word can offer you too support when you most need it.

Old Testament Words of Comfort

God's Promises to Mankind:

Be fruitful and increase in number; fill the earth and subdue it. Rule over the fish of the sea and the birds of the air and over every living creature that moves on the ground. (Genesis 1:28)

He who has clean hands and a pure heart, who does not lift up his soul to an idol, or swear by what is false, he will receive blessing from the Lord and vindication from God his savior. (Psalm 24:4-5)

He sent forth his word and healed them. (Psalm 107:20a)

He settles the barren women in her home as a happy mother of children. Praise the Lord. (Psalm 113:9)

Sons [daughters] are a heritage from the lord, children a reward from him. (Psalm 127:3)

Blessed are all who fear the Lord, who walk in his ways . . . Your wife will be like a fruitful vine within your house; your sons [daughters] will be like olive shoots around your table. Thus is the man [woman] blessed who fears the Lord. (Psalm 128:1, 3-4)

The righteous man [woman] leads a blameless life; blessed are his [her] children after him. (Proverbs 20:7)

But he was pierced for our transgressions; he was crushed for our iniquities; the punishment that brought us peace was upon him, and by his wounds we are healed. (Isaiah 53:5)

God's Promises to Abraham:

I will confirm my covenant between me and you and will greatly increase your numbers . . . I will make you very fruitful; I will make nations of you, and kings will come from you. (Genesis 17:2, 6)

As for Sarai your wife, you are no longer to call her Sarai; her name will be Sarah. I will bless her and will surely give you a son by her. I will bless her so that she will be the mother of nations; kings of peoples will come from her. (Genesis 17: 15-16).

And through your offspring all nations on earth will be blessed, because you have obeyed me. (Genesis 22:18)

God's Promise to Jacob:

Be fruitful and increase in number. A nation and a community of nations will come from you, and kings will come from your body. (Genesis 35:11)

God's Promises to Israel:

But the Israelites were fruitful and multiplied greatly and became exceedingly numerous, so that the land was filled with them. (Exodus 1:7).

And none will miscarry or be barren in your land, I will give you a full life span. (Exodus 23:26)

He will love you and bless you and increase your numbers. He will bless the fruit of your womb . .
. You will be blessed more than any other people; none of your men or women will be childless, nor any of your livestock without young. (Deuteronomy 7:13a-14)

All these blessings will come upon you and accompany you if you obey the lord your God . .
. The fruit of your womb will be blessed, and the crops of your land and the young of your livestock – the calves of your herds and the lambs of your flocks . . . The Lord will grant you abundant prosperity – in the fruit of your womb, the young of your livestock and the crops of your ground – in the land he swore to your forefathers to give you. (Deuteronomy 28:2-4, 11).

For I will pour water on the thirsty land, and streams on the dry ground; I will pour out my spirit on your offspring, and my blessing on your descendants. They will spring up like grass in the meadow, like poplar trees by flowing streams. (Isaiah 44:3-4)

Sing, O barren woman, you who never bore a child; burst into song, shout for you, you who were never in labor; because more are the children of the desolate woman than of her who has a husband, says the lord. Enlarge the place of your tent, stretch your tent curtains wide, do not hold back; lengthen your cords, strengthen your stakes. For you will spread out to the right and to the left; your descendants will dispossess nations and settle in their desolate cities. (Isaiah 54:1-3)

The Lord will call you back as if you were a wife deserted and distressed in spirit – a wife who married young, only to be rejected, says your God. For a brief moment I abandoned you, but with deep compassion I will bring you back. In a surge of anger I hid my face from you for a moment, but with everlasting kindness I will have compassion on you, says the Lord your redeemer. (Isaiah 54:6-8)

All your sons [daughters] will be taught by the lord, and great will be your children's peace. (Isaiah 54:13)

Come, let us return to the Lord. He has torn us to pieces but he will heal us; he has injured us but he will bind up our wounds. (Hosea 6:1)

Sing O Daughter of Zion, shout aloud, O Israel! Be glad and rejoice with all your heart, O Daughter of Jerusalem! The Lord has taken away your punishment, he has turned back your enemy. The Lord, the king of Israel, is with you; never again will you fear any harm. On that day they will say to Jerusalem, "Do not fear, O Zion; do not let your hands hang limp. The Lord your God is with you, he is mighty to save. He will take great delight in you, he will quiet you with his love, he will rejoice over you with singing." (Zephaniah 3:14-17)

Bring the whole tithe into the storehouse, that there may be food in my house. Test me in this, says the Lord almighty, and see if I will not throw open the floodgates of heaven and pour out so much blessing that you will not have room enough for it. I will prevent pests from devouring your crops, and the vines in your fields will not cast their fruit, says the Lord almighty. Then all the nations will call you blessed, for yours will be a delightful land, says the Lord almighty. (Malachi 3:10-12)

New Testament Words of Comfort

Words of Comfort from Jesus:

If you believe, you will receive whatever you ask for in prayer. (Matthew 21:22)

Ask and it will be given to you; seek and you will find; knock and the door will be opened to you. For everyone who asks receives; he who seeks finds; and to him who knocks, the door will be opened. (Matthew 7:7-8)

And I will do whatever you ask in my name, so that the son may bring glory to the father. You may ask me for anything in my name, and I will do it. (John 14:13-14)

If you remain in me and my words remain in you, ask whatever you wish, and it will be given you. This is my father's glory, that you bear much fruit, showing yourselves to be my disciples . . . You did not choose me, but I chose you and appointed you to go and bear fruit – fruit that will last. (John 15:7-8, 16)

Words of Blessing for all Believers

Blessed is she who has believed that what the Lord has said to her will be accomplished. (Luke 1:45)

Understand then, that those who believe are children of Abraham. The scripture foresaw that God would justify the gentiles by faith, and announced the gospel in advance to Abraham: "All nations will be blessed through you". So those who have faith are blessed along with Abraham, the man of faith. (Galatians 3:7-9)

Christ redeemed us from the curse of the law by becoming a curse for us, for it is written: "Cursed is everyone who is hung on a tree." He redeemed us in order that the blessing given to Abraham might come to the gentiles through Christ Jesus, so that by faith we might receive the promise of the Spirit. (Galatians 3:13-14)

But women will be saved through childbearing –
if they continue in faith, love and holiness with
propriety. (1 Timothy 2:15)

By faith Abraham, even though he was past age
– and Sarah herself was barren – was enabled to
become a father because he considered him
faithful who had made the promise. (Hebrews
11:11)

Dear friends, if our hearts do not condemn us, we
have confidence before God and receive from
him anything we ask, because we obey his
commands and do what pleases him. And this is
his command: to believe in the name of his son,
Jesus Christ, and to love one another as he
commanded us. Those who obey his commands
live in him, and he in them. And this is how we
know that he lives in us: We know it by the spirit
he gave us. (1 John 3:21-22)

And if we know that he hears us – whatever we ask – we know that we have what we asked of him. (1 John 5:15)

APPENDIX THREE:

My Prayer of Confession and Thanksgiving

"Our Father in Heaven, hallowed be your name, your kingdom come, your will be done on earth as it is in heaven. Give us today our daily bread. Forgive us our debts, as we also have forgiven our debtors. And lead us not into temptation, but deliver us from the evil one." – Matthew 6:9-13

Below is an example of the prayers of confession and thanksgiving I mentioned in Chapter Ten. If you feel led by the Spirit of God to do something similar, please take the time to ask God to reveal those areas in your life you specifically need to pray over.

My Prayer of Confession

Dear heavenly Father, I admit that I have been blind to the truth of your Word. I have allowed Satan to feed me lies of deception regarding my womanhood, which is truly a gift given to me by you. I renounce Satan's influence over my belief system and profess that Jesus is Lord and Master over all of my life. Therefore I choose to listen only to the truth that comes from the divinely inspired Word of God and through your Holy Spirit.

God, I confess I have spoken curses over my body, which is in direct contrast to your precious Word. Lord, I present to you the following words I have spoken regarding my reproductive system and fertility that are not life giving and for which I am truly sorry to have said:

- I am barren.

- I can't have children.

- I'm never going to be a mum.

- I get so sick with my periods.

- I don't ovulate regularly.

- I've got the dreaded curse again.

- I have endometriosis.

- I have unknown infertility.

- I hate being a girl.

Lord God, I recognize the damage I have done in speaking out these negative words over my body. I now renounce in the name of Jesus these and any other destructive lies I have spoken contrary to your truth. I pray that you will restore what I have harmed through my spoken words and that you will help me to guard my tongue, protecting me from further deception. I thank you for your cleansing and healing blood that has truly set me free in your Son Jesus's precious name. Amen.

My Prayer of Thanksgiving

Gracious Father, I thank you for your Word, which has truly set me free and revealed the truth about my fertility. I accept the blood and sacrifice your Son Jesus Christ offered for me, and I accept him as Lord and Savior over my life. I believe that Jesus has restored my fertility, which was stolen from me by the enemy and which I now claim back as my rightful inheritance as your daughter. I thank you that in your Word you have written these promises:

- None shall miscarry or be barren. (Exodus 23:26)

- The fruit of your womb shall be blessed. (Deuteronomy 28:4)

- Behold children are a heritage from the Lord. The fruit of the womb is his reward. (Psalm 127:3)

- Your wife shall be like a fruitful vine. In the very heart of your house, your children like olive plants all around your table. (Psalm 128:3)

I proclaim the truth of your Word over my body now and thank you, Lord Jesus, that by your blood I am healed. I believe that I am already a fruitful mother of children, and I accept this wonderful blessing as a gift from you and pledge that I will wait with expectancy for your perfect will in my life. In Jesus's name, I praise and thank you. Amen.

APPENDIX FOUR:

Eternal Life

"That if you confess with your mouth, Jesus is Lord, and believe in your heart that God raised him from the dead, you will be saved. For it is with your heart that you believe and are justified, and it is with your mouth that you confess and are saved."

—Romans 10:9-10

***

Having a relationship with Jesus Christ is the very best thing I have ever done. Without Jesus, none of my journey would have been possible. But more importantly, life without God the Father, his Son, and his Spirit would be a life void of meaning. It would also represent an eternal life separate from him.

If you haven't yet entered into a personal relationship with the God of the Universe, I encourage you to take this important step in your life. It is as simple as inviting Jesus into your life, confessing him as your Lord and believing he is the Son of God. Here is a wonderful example of a Salvation Prayer you can pray.

Prayer for Salvation

Lord Jesus, thank you for dying on the cross for me and taking away all my sins. By your blood offering I am now cleansed today and forever. I thank the Father for sending you, and I believe you are the Son of God who died on the cross, rose again, and are now seated at the right hand of our Father, preparing a home for me in heaven. I love you, Lord Jesus, and I thank you, Father, for sending the Holy Spirit to us after Jesus ascended into heaven. I give you my life and thank you for giving me eternal life. Amen.

Nurturing the Christian Walk

Once you have prayed this prayer, dear reader, I would also encourage you to start reading the Bible, the living word of God. The Bible is where truth will be revealed as Jesus himself stated:

I am the way and the truth and the life. (John 14:6)

The truth will set you free. (John 8:32)

To be nurtured in your Christian walk, it is also important to find a Bible-believing, Christ-centered, Spirit-filled church which can journey alongside you. It is very difficult to live out faith alone, so I truly encourage you to find someone who shares your faith beliefs who can journey this season with you.

About the Author

Nicole resides in country Victoria, Australia, with her husband Jamie, and three children, Faith, Joel, and Levi. Jamie and Nicole own and operate a residential and commercial building company in the Macedon Ranges whilst also managing their Pine Plantation on the outskirts of Woodend.

Nicole continues to write Christian literature and besides assisting in her family businesses, she also enjoys her ministry work at their local Baptist church.

Jamie and Nicole are both passionate about seeing the broken-hearted restored, and encouraging God's children to accept their true worth and value in him. After coming out of a cultish church upbringing, Jamie and Nicole both tried to *do* life their own way. It ended up messy! It was the unlikely *gift* of a nine-year barrenness season that led Nicole on a faith journey of her own, and ultimately brought a newfound intimate relationship with the Trinity of God.

It was during this time in the wilderness that Nicole learnt to worship, trust, and desire God more than anything else. And it was out of a long and arduous barrenness experience that God realigned her thinking, and ultimately brought restoration and victory in every area of her life that needed His healing touch.

If you have enjoyed Nicole's story and would like her to pray for you, or if you would simply like to get in touch with her, please visit: https://www.nicolezoch.com/

Lightning Source UK Ltd.
Milton Keynes UK
UKHW021814200519
343003UK00015B/250/P

9 781644 406540